844

25.

LHASA,
THE OPEN CITY

LHASA,
THE OPEN CITY
A Journey to Tibet

Han Suyin

G. P. PUTNAM'S SONS
NEW YORK

FIRST AMERICAN EDITION, 1977

Copyright © 1977 by Han Suyin

A French version of this book was
published under the title *Lhassa,
Etoile-Fleur* by Editions Stock in 1976.

SBN: 399-12035-1

Library of Congress Catalog Number 77-9379

PRINTED IN THE UNITED STATES OF AMERICA

Contents

Illustrations

Following page 84

Photographs taken by the author

Preface and Acknowledgments

The title, *Lhasa, The Open City*, seems a contradiction with the impression of a secret, hermetic Tibet, which allows no visitors.

But it is not so today. Just as India has recently allowed visitors into Northern Kashmir, after twenty-nine years of keeping it forbidden territory, so China is now allowing a stream of visitors to Tibet.

Since my visit in October–November 1975, a small spate of visitors has gone to this once forbidden region. In January 1976 the Mexican Ambassador and his wife on their way home travelled through Lhasa, where they spent five days. In June His Majesty King Birendra of Nepal, with a retinue of journalists and officials, travelled through Tibet to return to his own country. In July two Englishmen, Felix Greene and Neville Maxwell, went to Tibet, and they were closely followed by Princess Ashraf Pahlavi, sister of the Shah of Iran. The Danish Ambassador to Peking, and his wife, also visited Tibet some time in June. And more visitors are going there now.

Although amenities are still scanty (there are no hotels and no restaurants) and therefore the flow of visitors is limited, the Chinese Government have decided to open Tibet. The changes which have taken place will therefore become better known. And amenities for visitors promise to become improved in the future.

In my book, which is a survey of the changes in Tibet, in all sectors, I have quoted, here and there, from visitors ranging through the nineteenth and twentieth centuries. Their observations enabled me to check up on what has been transformed and what has not—for Tibet changed very little through the millennia, right up until 1959. To the late Stuart Gelder and his wife Roma, who visited Tibet in 1963–4, and to their book, *The Timely Rain*, I owe a great deal, for they were there at a period of transition between old and new.

Finally, I wish to thank the Chinese Government, and also all my friends in Tibet, who looked after me so well, and made available to me so much material, without in any way trying to convince me or to change my own views.

HAN SUYIN

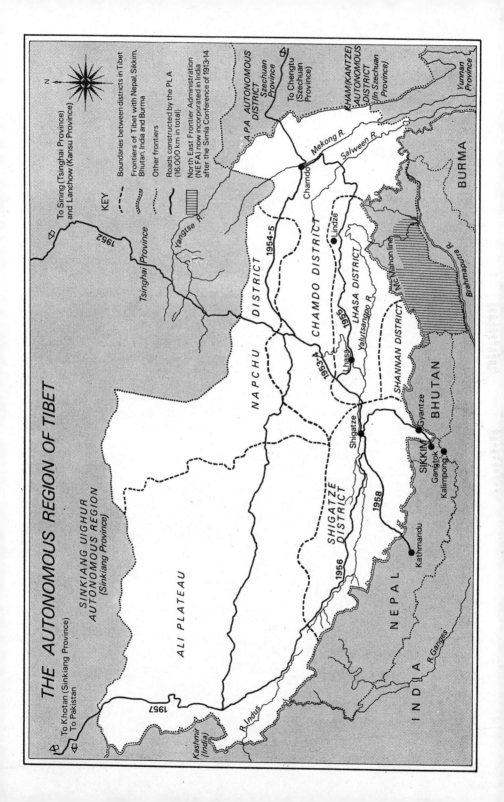

1

Tibet and the Time Machine

October in Lhasa. At seven in the morning sunrise is a dense pink glow beyond the 6,000-foot high Tangla hills flanking the valley. The gold-clad roofs of Lhasa's temples and sanctuaries wink awake. Bicycles whir upon the smooth tarmac avenue in front of the guesthouse, and leave slim tracks in the dew. Tibetan boys and girls in fur caps, plimsolls and padded cotton jackets jostle each other. A lorry purrs. A horseman wrapped in pale leather, his loose right sleeve dangling, sings to his horse's canter. Along the tree-lined avenue women go smooth upon silent feet, their dark gowns sway, and laughter — marvellous Tibetan laughter — escapes from under their hoods. It is still below zero degree, but in another hour the sun will leap into a sudden blue sky, and shake the whole city into light and warmth. Morning comes to Lhasa two hours later than in Peking, 6,000 kilometres farther east. But Lhasa time is Peking time, as it is all over China. To the farthest end of China only one time prevails, and there is no winding back and forth of watches in obedience to the meridians or to the sun.

Am I really in Lhasa? For the last twenty years, following China's galloping revolution, I have adapted to an accelerating time machine pelting through centuries to reach the present and then over-reaching today in a headlong hunt of the future. But in Lhasa I feel a touch of nostalgia, searching for what is gone. I hear the bells of yak herds outside the unwalled city — in the rarefied, crystal-pure air, sound, vision, smell, are all enhanced — I also hear the lorries in convoy growling as they churn the white sand roads which radiate from Lhasa — 2,800 kilometres east to Szechuan, 2,500 kilometres north to Kansu, 5,000 kilometres west and north to Sinkiang — 1,200 kilometres to Kathmandu. I know that yesterday's secret, hermetic Tibet is gone for ever. It never was a fabulous Shangri-la. Not for me. Nor for my father or grandfather. Least of all, for the Tibetans themselves.

My family comes from Szechuan, Tibet's close neighbour province. We share a common border and also people, and for over two centuries, my family engaged in the tea trade — brick tea — to Tibet.

Szechuan is in two parts: its eastern region a flat, sea-level plain, enormously fertile; its western region mountainous, part of the giant staircase system which here coiled and plicated the earth, and which finally thrust into the air, some million years ago, the enormous Himalayas and also the Tibetan plateau, whose average height is three kilometres in the sky. The eastern plain of Szechuan is predominantly Han Chinese[1] — and many of the Hans have come, in great migrations since the twelfth century, from other provinces of China, driven there by the invasions of the Mongols and the Manchus.[2] In the west, among the mountains, Hans are also found, but many ethnic groups, such as the Yis of the Cool Mountains, the Miaos round Mount Omei, inhabit higher land, and two large districts, the Apa and the Kantze or Khampa,[3] are predominantly peopled by Tibetans. These two districts alone make up around 35 per cent of the area of Szechuan (area 560,000 square kilometres) but contain less than 2 per cent of its inhabitants (90 million or slightly more). Of these 2 per cent some 60 to 70 per cent are Tibetan, or Tsang, as they are called in China.

In the past, we often saw in Chengtu, capital city of Szechuan province, Tibetan lords high-booted and fur-robed, who came to purchase ornaments, silks and embroideries, brocade, and porcelain. The city has a Tibetan quarter, established for some centuries. In its shops one could buy pale blue or white silk *hattas* — long slim scarves proffered ceremonially as gifts when visiting Tibetan officials. Pilgrims to Lhasa offered them when supplicating the deities in the temples.

By 1975 hattas were no longer to be found in Chengtu shops, but there were still boots, red and black, or white and embroidered; wooden bowls, sometimes silver encrusted, which Tibetans always carry with them and in which they eat their staple tsampa — grilled barley, tea and yak butter mixed in an odorous mash — trilby felt hats, headgear of all Tibetan males including the lama-priests; fur hats with fox tails wound round the brim; women's embroidered caps; women's aprons of heavy hand-made wool in red, white and green stripes with sashes of brocade round the waist; turquoise necklaces, and coral jewellery.

There was my uncle, a huge man with a stentorian voice which made the window panes quiver; he was called a 'lolo', nickname in Szechuan for some Tibetans. He came from western Szechuan, and lived to ninety-four, and loved to climb mountains.

In 1941, during the Sino-Japanese war, the Chinese government of Chiang Kai-shek was installed in Chungking, Szechuan's largest city after Chengtu. There I met the Tibetan delegation which had come to the Bureau of Tibetan Affairs. They had travelled on horseback, a six-week journey then, to seek the approval of Chiang Kai-shek for the investiture of a new Dalai Lama. For, traditionally, Tibet being part of China, the authority of the Chinese government was required before any high functionary, a Dalai Lama or a Panchen Lama, supreme pontiffs of the Tibetan religious-secular hierarchy, could assume their functions and be officially installed.

Tibet, then, to us in Szechuan, was no strange land; it was Sitsang, the western Tsang. We called it colloquially 'the inland'. And when I reached Lhasa, I found that Tibetans spoke of Szechuan, and other provinces of China, as 'the inland'.

I had come, aware of change, but unaware of how much Tibet had changed. Yet here, as all over China, accelerated metamorphosis was going on; I would see the time machine gather speed, and space, that great beast, laid low by human toil. And this was a miracle greater than all reputed divine agencies could muster.

In July 1966 I had obtained permission to visit Tibet, and arrived in August in Chengtu, take-off point not only for the 2,800 kilometre road to Lhasa, but also for twice-weekly planes. By 1975, there were six weekly flights to Lhasa from Chengtu, and four more from Lanchow, in Kansu province.

I did not reach Lhasa in 1966, for the Cultural Revolution was astir. The streets of Chengtu were filled with a million singing, sloganing inhabitants. They beat drums, clashed cymbals, flew thousands of vermilion flags.

Every morning for a week I went to Chengtu airport. The Lhasa-bound plane was poised on the tarmac; it revved hopefully, once even took a limbering stroll down the runway. The airport manager—who had been a PLA man, ten years in Tibet—courteously played gin rummy with me while waiting for a takeoff ... which did not happen. After an hour or so the pilots would emerge from the cockpit and walk towards us. 'The storm has not abated. No going today.' 'Perhaps tomorrow', the airport manager would reply, gathering up the card pack. 'Come tomorrow.' It took me seven days to realize that the Cultural Revolution was part of this obdurate storm; an unyielding climatic distemper which was reaching Tibet as well. With infinite politeness the airport manager saw me into a plane bound for Shanghai. 'Better luck next time.' And so it was, for in 1975, in Peking, in a jesting mood, I said: 'I have now visited almost every part of China, including Sinkiang; I have been to both ends of the Great Wall, from the sea to the Gate of Propitious Rain in the Gobi desert; there remains Tibet.' 'To Tibet you shall go,' was the answer. I was unprepared, with only five rolls of Kodak film. But I went.

In the next few days much telephoning to Lhasa took place, for the assent of the local authorities of the Autonomous Region of Tibet was necessary. Connections by plane or train to 'the inland' of Szechuan are not easy to obtain, for there is a frenzy of travel and activity, of which the world knows little, going on all the time in China's interior provinces. Trains and planes are jam-packed and booked weeks ahead. Every main city hospital has 60 per cent of its personnel in the country-side; medical teams – 100–200 doctors, surgeons, biologists, laboratory assistants, nurses–range the vast land from the Altai mountains to the Himalayas, training barefoot doctors (1,300,000 of them in China now), establishing clinics, over-hauling the medical web in the countryside. Barefoot doctors also travel, coming to city hospitals for further training, or to attend regional conferences. Peasants by the thousand pack trains to go to other provinces and view agricultural innova-tions; students in great droves (12 million youngsters are estab-lished in rural areas) board trains and planes; they are loaded with enormous packs, much of it equipment and books they bring with them to new rural factories, schools and cultural centres; workers in serried ranks squeeze into trains and planes, going north-west, west and south-west where new in-dustrial cities are born. Geologists, chemists, meteorologists, seismologists, archaeologists ... travel to remote regions to prospect, gather material, set up scientific research centres. On railway stations groups with flags and drums greet other groups come to 'exchange experience' ... China is vitality abounding, and the farther inland one goes, the more obvious this becomes. When an 'honoured guest' travels, therefore, much work and planning goes into arranging a smooth, effi-cient passage to his destination.

I was back in Chengtu in October 1975, and no storm loomed on the horizon. The Chengtu plain was muffled in its autumn fog. A moonfaced sun peered once, gave up, and was swallowed in the thick mist. The day's substance dissolved until all things became their own impalpable ghosts. At night I heard the soil. That glistening, glutinous black earth of my province, into which so much sweat, toil and dung of man in his millions has gone through the centuries, heaved and

2

muttered with life. Everything was relentlessly viscous; towels always damp, clothes washed did not dry; and the moss grew visibly, audibly, until I felt it carpeted even my inner ears.

Once again to Chengtu airport, wading through the marshmallow early morning. Twenty yards away the plane, an Ilyushin 14, was only a pale glimmer. Filing into it were cadres, in military uniform, in civilian clothes; workers and agricultural technicians, a medical team from Hunan going to Tibet for two years; women, one even with a young child – a rarity, for lowland children do not thrive in Tibet. The packed plane took off punctually as I waved at the fog which contained the shadows of my sixth brother and his wife, and relatives and friends.

The flight took two hours twenty minutes. We burst above the fog blanket, and everyone said 'Aah' and bent to the plane windows to see the beautiful thrust of Miniagangka and its smaller brother, in Chinese called 'the two princeling peaks', conical perfections. Other snow mountains now peopled the horizon, among them a distant, glacial fortress, like that of some magic ice-kingdom, a massive quadrilateral studded with diamond peaks like some enormous jewelled brooch pinned on to the skyline. The fog ocean below us was neatly scissored away by a high range and we were flying over the Chamdo area of Tibet. Range upon range of brown, windswept mountains, sloped forested sprawls to deep gorges where emerald water flowed. The headwaters of Asia's great rivers, the Yangtze, the Salween, and the Mekong, all squeeze down mountain corridors from this part of Tibet. The plane cabin was well pressurized (we flew at 24,000 feet).

Apple-cheeked and attentive, the hostess distributed tea and fruit. She had flown the Lhasa–Chengtu run for three years. 'One never gets tired of the sight of mountains.' Then we were coming down into Lhasa airport, 3,800 metres above sea-level, and landed without a bump. 'Be careful, comrades, do not rush out, you may find it hard to breathe.' Outside, on the apron, were buses waiting to drive passengers the 110 kilometres to Lhasa city. The airport was a small plain, hill-cupped, new planted with slim-boled ash trees and poplars; the airport building nondescript grey brick, similar to so many in China. A white sand road stretched ahead. I looked up. A sky so blue, it was almost black. So perfect and smoothly blue-black, I was suddenly conscious of the earth being a small round ball suspended in space. If levitation exists, I felt levitated by the sight of immense space to plunge in, vertigo in reverse.

'Welcome, welcome.' I shook hands with my hosts from the Friendship Association, Tibetan branch, and the Lhasa revolutionary committee. Among my welcomers was a slim young Tibetan woman with two neat pigtails, Dr Chasi. She held under her arm an oxygen pillow with a trailing rubber tube for nostril insertion. It was for me. Solicitously, Madame Chen—efficient, from Shanghai, more than fifteen years in Tibet, and who arranged all my interviews and visits—enquired about my health while pouring green tea. Did I feel shaky? Tremulous? The onset of headache, giddiness, dizziness, panting, cramps, nausea? Tactfully my hosts forbore to mention irritability, a well-known symptom of oxygen lack, and one which Stuart Gelder suffered—or inflicted upon others to bear—when in Tibet in 1962.[4]

I expatiated upon my good health. Before leaving Chengtu I had had a rigorous medical examination. My electrocardiogram was inspected inch by inch by a well-known cardiologist there. For Tibet up in the sky is a strain upon heart and lungs. Even vigorous, hardy people may contract altitude sickness, for which the only remedy is swift evacuation to lower levels. It takes a week or more, even for Tibetans who sojourn some months in lower lands, to get re-accustomed to the rarefied air. I was expected, when in Lhasa, to take to my bed and to be out of action for some days.

But I did spectacularly well. I did not pant, and save for a blistering headache the first night—which arrived at 2 a.m. and left me promptly at 6 a.m.—suffered no inconvenience.

But then I did *not* go to bed; instead, in the hot noonday sun, I paced the courtyard in front of the guesthouse for an hour or two, warming my muscles, breathing slow and deep. And, twenty-four hours after reaching Lhasa, I was fit and went on to feel better than I had ever done in my whole life. This renewed, exhilarating vitality, I was to keep for weeks after I went down again. Perhaps, in a previous incarnation, I was a mountain goat ...

'You are indeed a vigorous old lady,' remarked my hosts. The oxygen pillow went untouched save for the first night. 'Like a fish in water,' was another remark; both immensely flattering. Old age (I am near sixty) is still high praise in China. I put it down to my recipe: not bed, but a gentle walk, teaching the body to like what it gets in oxygen, and that very promptly.

Gold and turquoise, turquoise and gold. As we drove the 110 kilometres to Lhasa in a Shanghai sedan, all was piercing vision, lapidary sight. First the hills flanking the valley; such satin smooth, naked golden hills! By the motor road at their foot also ran the river Kyi, tributary of the Yalutsangpo. The Yalutsangpo is actually the upper reach of the Brahmaputra river, which later turns round a knob of the Himalayas and waters the Indian plains and plunges through the delta where the Ganges also issues into the Bay of Bengal. But here the Yalutsangpo is pure sapphire, its stream interspersed with water meadows upon which graze sheep, jet-black yaks, cows and horses. Yak-skin coracles were moored by the water's edge, and on the farther side, so near as to seem graspable, were white, neat, flat-roofed village houses with shorn fields about them, great sheaves of golden barley and mudwalled enclosures of young trees. Along the road came a horseman or two, with high boots and plumed trilbies, who reared in their saddles in salute. Some women in striped aprons were sweeping the motor road, they smiled and waved and cheered. We passed a dozen lorries going to Lhasa. And after the first 100 kilometres I suddenly realized: how few the people on the road!

How small the villages, no more than ten or twelves house to each! How few the people in the fields! How stark, how bare, the land!

Coming from the provinces of China where the eye is never free of people on the road, in horsecarts, trucks, in the villages, people working in the fields by the hundred, the first – and abiding, and subsequently confirmed – impression here is: how few the people!

'There are three great lacks in Tibet: fuel, communication, and people,' said Comrade Chen. 'And there were three abundances before. Poverty, oppression, and the terror of the supernatural. The three latter caused the former.'

We drove past great Buddhas of stone carved in the hill slopes. Here pilgrims plodding to Lhasa (and some, in a medieval piety similar to that of Europe in the Dark Ages, or of India today, did the whole journey prostrating themselves at every step), used to place their first offerings. We went over a new bridge spanning the river, past fields where barley heaped great honey-coloured stacks and the new winter wheat laid down a pale green carpet. Then, at last, from 15 kilometres away, came the vision that has been for centuries fulfilment of heart's desire, promise of a better life in the next reincarnation for so many: on a high hill, looking as if it floated in air, majestic and awesome in its perfection, the Potala, with glittering golden roofs above its massive white walls, a castle upon a fortress upon a mountain. The Potala, erstwhile abode of the pontiff-ruler of Tibet, the Dalai Lama. No one can remain unmoved by the sheer power and beauty of the structure, with its thousand windows like a thousand eyes staring at the sun. It totally absorbed sight and attention, dwarfing its surroundings, and the city of Lhasa below it looked like a small village, so great was the mass of the Potala towering above it.

For the next ten days, my eyes would turn to it, pink morning, white-hot noon and amethyst evening, to watch it watching the valley at its feet, until I had explored it, and turned away from its monster beauty with rancour and nausea.

And now we entered Lhasa: a smooth, tarred avenue lined by poplars wind-dancing gold and silver leaves led straight into it. No walls, no gates, no suburbs. At first sight a nondescript, clean new city: new buildings of brick, such as everywhere in China: post office, cinema, shops, an emporium, a revolutionary museum, a sports stadium, a hospital, new apartment houses. All neat, all functional. Lorries, bicycles, people walking the tree-shaded sidewalks; some in boots and Tibetan wool or leather gowns, belted at the waist to form a kangaroo pouch at the breast — in which everything goes, pet dogs, babies, food, the tsampa bowl. Others, younger, in cotton padded jackets and khaki trousers and workers' caps. Here and there a few Han Chinese, not many.

I stay at the official guesthouse where, in September 1975, the delegation from the Central Government, headed by Mr Hua Kuo-feng, China's recent Prime Minister, came to celebrate the tenth anniversary of the Tibet Autonomous Region of China (first proclaimed in September 1965). There are no hotels in Lhasa, and no restaurants — anyway Tibetan cooking does not exist. The guesthouse rooms are about twenty in number. They are clean and comfortable when not facing north, for here one broils in the noonday sun, and freezes in the shade. There are bathrooms to each room, but only cold water. Fuel scarcity is a constant factor, and the Hans, military or civilian, do not heat their rooms, even in winter, preferring to set an example. Only the high prelates, the nobles, used to heat their houses with charcoal braziers, and for this an army of serfs and slaves used to gather wood and bring it to the monasteries and the palaces. There is a public bath house, where hot water is available, heated by a solar converter to save fuel. Twice in the next ten days I would shower, but one does not feel a compulsion to wash much in Tibet, and perhaps that is why daily ablutions remain, for Tibetans, a novel enterprise. 'But the young are learning to wash as we do,' says Madame Chen to me.

However it be, washing here irritates the skin and berefts it of natural oils, most necessary screen against the lethal ultra-violet rays of the sun.

From my room I see the living quarters of cadres employed in the administrative offices of Lhasa. Here Hans and Tibetans live side by side, in similar flats. Every morning I see them go to the communal kitchen and come back with Thermos flasks filled with hot water, and morning, noon and night with hot dishes, from the canteen. Below my window 200 enormous cabbages (vegetables here grow outsize) lie dehydrating in the sun, to be eaten in winter. A little farther, by a heap of stones, six Tibetan women and four Tibetan men are breaking, with much joy and total lack of frenzy, the stones to pave another small road. They laugh and sing, and from time to time a splendid Tibetan man appears with a handcart and carts the stones away. But again, how few people, how few, for all this enormous space! I walk into the avenue and turn into another similar avenue, and there, right before me, is the old city of Lhasa, a great dazzle of shining golden roofs at its heart, rows of whitewashed, flat-roofed houses with gaily painted windows and flower pots everywhere, and painted door lintels. And again, so few, so few the people!

And for this lack of people, in this great space that is Tibet, with 1,220,000 square kilometres, over twice the size of my province of Szechuan, who is to blame? To answer this, a look at history is necessary.

Tibet's history begins in the year A.D. 640, when the region of U (Central Tibet, with Lhasa as its nucleus) was unified under a King, Songtsang Kampo, who came from Tzetang, in southern Tibet. Even today, Tibet is far from homogeneous; there are five ethnic groups, the Tsang or Tibetan proper, the Memba, Loba, the Khampa (from the western area of Szechuan),[5] and the Hui, or Islamic Tibetans, for there is a mosque in Lhasa. In features too, one can see variety: some Tibetans look almost Burmese; others Mongolian; yet others have Persian features, denoting an Afghan or Persian ancestry.

The word Tibet (Tu-Bu) first appears on Chinese maps of the Tang dynasty; the people were also called Tufan, a name which seems to cover a variable area. Later they are mixed up with the Tangut nomads from North Tibet, who are a nomadic Altaic tribe with whom Tibetans in the pastoral regions of northern Tibet seem to have merged. In fact, Tibetans are still called Tanguts in Tsinghai province.

King Songtsang Kampo was only twenty-three in A.D. 640, but a most gifted, energetic and wise statesman. He is said to have unified weights and measures, and with his able Prime Minister created an alphabet for the Tsang (Tibetan) language spoken round Lhasa, deriving its 30 letters from old Sanskrit. A warrior as well, he established a class of armed noblemen, who owed him allegiance, and sought alliances with his powerful neighbour, the Chinese Tang dynasty. He married in A.D. 641 a Chinese princess, the princess Wen Cheng, adopted daughter of the Chinese emperor Tai Tsung. He also married a Nepalese princess,[6] and furthermore had a Tibetan wife. Princess Wen Cheng, intelligent and beautiful, brought Buddhism to Tibet; the King was converted and his people would follow suit.[7]

Previously Tibet had a religion, called Bon, a form of animistic nature worship. Bon never totally disappeared. It was to infiltrate and distort Tibetan Buddhism in its later development, so that shamanism, sorcery, witchcraft became incorporated in religion as it was practised among the people.

Princess Wen Cheng, thirteen centuries later, is still revered among Tibetans. One example is the Feast of Flowers, as told by Père Huc in his travels.[8] At the great monastery of Kumbum, he attended this feast, at which great numbers of effigies carved out of butter, and coloured, represented the voyage of Princess Wen Cheng from China to Tibet to marry Songtsang Kampo. Stuart Gelder, who passed through Tsinghai province on his way to Tibet, found in 1962 another such effigy of melting butter and photographed it.[9] All over Tibet, shrines to the Good Princess, and ex-votos in the Jokka Kang, the holiest temple of all in Tibet, at the heart of Lhasa, testify to this veneration. Wen Cheng brought with her a large statue of the Buddha, said to have been miraculously created. Made of an alloy of gold, silver and bronze, this Buddha is still today in the Jokka Kang. In fact the temple itself was built to commemorate her arrival.

Songtsang Kampo was eager to emulate the skills and cultural attainments of the Chinese empire; and at his request Wen Cheng brought with her thousands of artisans and craftsmen, architects and teachers and cooks, carpenters and painters. Again in A.D. 710 another Princess, Tsing Cheng, married another Tibetan king, and brought with her musicians and dancers, bolts of silk and brocade and spinners. The love of Tibetans for Chinese silk dates from then, and Tibetans were sent to China to study paper making, ceramics, and other crafts. The Kings of Tibet also adopted the 'Tang law', which remained in force in Tibet (though subsequently much distorted by the religious hierarchy which took power) until 1949.

Under its first two powerful monarchs, Tibet became a strong military state. According to records, the population at its apogee in the tenth century reached 10–12 millions. Tibetan raiding forces spread into west India, upper Burma, Yunnan, Szechuan, Kansu and into Tsinghai, occupying a vast area; hence today the enclaves of Tibetans in five provinces of China, and overlapping the Himalayas into Sikkim, Bhutan, and northern India and Kashmir. So vigorous was their martial prowess that they even invested Chang An, the capital of the Tang empire, for a short while. And then decline began. Tibet disintegrated from within; and one of the factors of this disintegration was the Buddhist religion imported by King Songtsang Kampo to promote unification.

For here religion flourished. Tibet is a land of valleys, cut off from each other by high mountains. While the military-nobleman caste went out to war, the monasteries became powerful; they were the repositories of knowledge, and became the largest landlords. They also were the places where there were large concentrations of able-bodied men, and levies of armed bands were kept by each monastery, while the central power, torn by internecine feuds—such as occurred in medieval Europe—grew weak. The monasteries waxed strong and challenged the monarchy. In the tenth century Lang Darma, last of the lay kings, made an effort to curb priestly power, but he was assassinated and Tibet split into factions, with religious sects also waging wars. A mixed lay and clerical hierarchy now took over, as the sons of the nobility, to strengthen themselves, became prelates of the Buddhist church. Thus began the rise of this unique theocratic absolutism, which would keep Tibet unchanged, closed to outside influence until the middle of the twentieth century.

In those centuries Tibetan Buddhism evolved its own particular features: a mixture of the old Bon religion, with added features of Hinduism and Tantrism. Lamaism—as we shall now call it—spread to the advancing hordes of nomadic tribesmen from the steppes of central Asia who were on the move from the tenth century onwards and began their formidable advance into China's plains. The Tang Empire was overthrown in A.D. 907, not only through the assault of these fierce invaders who came in waves (Uighurs, Tadjiks, Tatars) but also because of the large peasant revolts which plagued it, such as that of Huang Chao and Wang Hsien-chih (A.D. 874–84).

The conflicts which followed fragmented both China and Tibet until the rise of the Mongols. These nomads and hunters used iron to make weapons and tools, and organized a powerful cavalry, the key factor in their enormous conquests. By A.D. 1206 Temujin their chief had consolidated all the Mongolian tribes under his leadership and became Genghis Khan (the Great Khan). His conquest of China was completed by his grandson Kublai Khan, who became Emperor of the Chinese Yuan dynasty, with its seat at Cambulic, today's Peking.

In 1260 Kublai Khan invited to Peking the leader of Tibetan lamaism, Basba, pontiff of the Sakya religious sect, who was striving for supremacy. Basba, a forceful and ambitious man, went to Peking, where he performed 'miracles' unmatched by other wise men in a great contest, and converted a great many Mongolian princes to Lamaism. He was appointed 'tutor to the Emperor', with rule over 130,000 families in Tibet as far as Lake Kokonor. He also created an alphabet for the Mongolian language, which had no writing. In return for being invested with power, both secular and religious, in Tibet, he paid homage to Kublai Khan as his vassal, and Tibet became officially part of the Chinese Yuan empire.[10]

Even today, Ngapo Nawang Jigme, a Tibetan aristocrat once minister to the Dalai Lama, but who did not join in the Tibetan insurrection of 1959 and who is now vice-chairman of the standing committee of the National Congress of China, as well as chairman of the Autonomous Region of Tibet, claims that he is descended from Tibetan aristocrats selected by Kublai Khan, and states that Tibet became part of 'the mother country in the time of Kublai Khan'.

The backing of the Yuan emperors permitted lamaism to flourish, not only in Tibet, but also among the Mongols; it was now impossible for lay kings to rise and to abolish it.

A century later Tsong Kapa, another powerful prelate, began a reform movement among the Tibetan clergy to purge it from evil practices, corruption and devil worship.

Celibacy was enforced; as well as the wearing of high conical hats, resembling the Christian bishop's mitre, and other ceremonies and practices, many of which, as Winnington points out[11] (and as Père Huc[12] also noticed), bear a great resemblance to catholic rites and practices of those days. Since the Yuan court admitted many foreigners (and used them as officials to rule the restive Han Chinese), it is possible that Tsong Kapa did come at the time in contact with Christians at the Mongol court.

The new reformed sect, called Gelugpa or Yellow-hat sect to distinguish it from the Sakya or Red-hatted sect, throve greatly. Monasteries were built and strengthened as fortresses, with standing armies in each, and the holy writings and canons were also overhauled and consigned to parchment. I saw some of these, well preserved in the Drepung monastery in Lhasa today.

But enforced celibacy brought up the problem of succession to religious pontiffs. That is when the Buddhist theory of reincarnation was incorporated within the power system. The soul of the Great Lama, upon his death, entered another body, that of a baby born at the exact time when the pontiff expired. Thus succession of the incarnate spirit transcending successive bodies was assurance of religious continuity. It was at the time of the Fifth Great Lama, a man of extraordinary energy and power, named Ngawang Lobsang, that reincarnation became absolute doctrine (around 1475). The Great Fifth, as he is known, became the first one on whom the title of Dalai Lama, meaning Ocean of Wisdom, was officially conferred (the first four then became retroactively Dalai Lamas). Under the Great Fifth the long struggle for supremacy in Tibet ended with the total merger of religious and secular rule, but with the religious prelate always superior to the lay officials.

And now it was easy to obtain 'bodies' for reincarnation. To replenish its ranks the clergy contracted alliances with the old aristocracy and the landlords, whose sons now went into monasteries to become high prelates. This concatenation was 'the three great masters', as the Tibetans called the hierarchy which ruled them.

Reincarnation was the core of lama power. Care was taken, however, that the souls of the Dalai and Panchen Lamas should re-enter the world in the bodies of children of lowly families and not of noble ones, to ensure that no single lay family of any influence should seize the title and make it hereditary. The family of the discovered reincarnation was granted a dukedom, and all members of the family raised to the nobility.

When a Dalai Lama dies, search for his child successor begins: born at the time the spirit departed its previous 'body'. Dreams and signs and portents come to the prelates appointed to find him. Prayer and devotion, gazing at cloud formation above a certain holy lake in Tibet, reveal images which help to locate the house where the future God-King is born … in a cow-byre or a stable. All women in Tibet, bar the wealthiest and noblest, always gave birth in cow-byres. The young child is submitted to many tests, such as recognizing objects belonging to the previous Dalai Lama. Occasionally controversy arises, two children being found who fulfil the requirements. This happened in the case of the present Panchen Lama, the tenth in number. Two children were found, both among Tibetans outside Tibet, and it was up to Chairman Mao, finally, to decide, in the traditional manner.[13] As for the present Dalai Lama, born in 1935 in Tsinghai province, agreement had to be secured from the Kuomintang government of Chiang Kai-shek.[14] He was taken to Lhasa under armed escort of Chiang's troops, and his formal installation was approved by a minister appointed by Chiang.

The Institution of the Panchen Lama also dates back to the Great Fifth. The latter had a dream in which he was told that he was the reincarnation of Avalokiteshvara (in Tibetan Chenrezi), while his old tutor was the reincarnation of Amitaba Buddha, in Tibetan Opame. This makes the Panchen Lama somewhat spiritually superior to the Dalai, as Opame and Chenrezi have a father–son relationship. But all this is so mystical, and wrapped in such profundity of Buddhist apologetica, that even today experts dispute their meaning, since Chenrezi and Opame are also different aspects of the same Buddha incarnation. More practically, the Dalai Lama governed 109 counties and the Panchen Lama only 10; the former was installed in Lhasa, and the second in Shigatze. Whoever is older helps direct the search for the other. In reality, conflict and hostility between the two were frequent.

Reincarnation now became general, giving rise to numerous 'living Buddhas' who had chosen this world of sorrows in order to regenerate it, rather than the Bliss of Nirvana. Almost every noble family, and certainly those of many prelates, contained 'living Buddhas', not only in Tibet, but also in Mongolia. The system worked well; it prevented splits in pontiff power: it perpetuated a tenacious, obscurantist theocracy which looked upon change of any kind as a threat to its existence. While in Europe the Renaissance was heralded by the break-up of the Holy Roman Empire, in Tibet theocracy consolidated with the centuries. As in medieval Europe the priesthood strenuously opposed scientific experiments, and burnt as sorcerers those who propounded new theories about the universe, so the Buddhist Vatican of Lhasa would seclude Tibet and allow nothing new of any kind, and especially no lay education which would be a threat to their total control of minds.

But threat could also come from within: thus the Great Fifth's successor, the Sixth Dalai Lama, was a romantic, uxorious young man, and a poet; his songs – which were about women and love – delighted the people but shook the Establishment. He frequented brothels, and took women into the Potala. He was quietly removed and probably strangled. Four more Dalai Lamas between the Sixth and the present Fourteenth were to die young in mysterious fashion. Removal by assassination, within the many-chambered Potala, was not difficult, since the Dalai Lama chosen was a child, and before his official installation at the age of eighteen had to undergo severe fasting for a week. During his adolescence a Regent was usually appointed, and this also led to power struggles within the priesthood.

After the death of the Sixth a rift did occur; and an invasion by nomads from Dzungaria then took place. Lhasa was occupied, and the hierarchy appealed to its protector, the Chinese Emperor Kang Hsi (A.D. 1662–1723) who sent an army and expelled the invaders. By 1720 Dalai Lama succession was restored, and a Chinese viceroy, or Ampan, resided in Lhasa. Further dissension led the Emperor Chien Lung (1736–96) to specify that all appointments of importance in Tibet must be ratified by the Imperial Court; Chien Lung set up a Tibetan cabinet of ministers, called the Kashag, under the supervision of the Chinese viceroy, and abolished the office of regent to the Dalai Lama.

The Imperial Edict, and a golden vase in which the names of potential ministers were placed, to be drawn out by the Chinese viceroy, are on the topmost floor of the Potala Palace, and every New Year, the Dalai Lama was to bow low before it, in token of recognition of Chinese sovereignty over Tibet.

In 1789 the Gurkhas, who had conquered Nepal, invaded Tibet. Chien Lung again sent an army and drove them out, and stone obelisks were set up in Lhasa (they are still there) to commemorate the event.

But by then India was becoming 'British India', part of the British Empire which would reach its zenith of power and extent within the next fifty years. Thus the borders of Tibet were to be confronted with a new power, and this would lead to historical events which have a bearing today upon the relations between the present two largest Asian states, India and China. For the past is not easily got rid of, and also shapes our tomorrows.

Very effectively, time had been made to stop in Tibet; it would stay stopped until 1950. Comparison of the accounts of Père Huc, in Tibet in 1846, of Fosco Maraini, in Tibet in the 1920s,[15] and of other travellers, in the 1930s and later, all produce almost identical accounts. Nothing had changed or would change.

This total theocracy resulted in the most terrifying exploitation and impoverishment of the Tibetan people. It kept them in total ignorance, terrorized them into total submission.

The result was a swift decline in the population, a decline most marked, as Winnington writes, since the seventeenth century.[16]

The Han Chinese have been accused by certain irresponsible journalists, basing themselves on distorted reports, of 'genocide' in Tibet. One of these went so far as to accuse the Hans of murdering '3 million Tibetans'. This is said to have occurred after 1950, and the entry of the PLA (People's Liberation Army) in Tibet. The facts are different. As we have seen, there were round about 10–12 million Tibetans, in the eastern part of Tibet alone, ten centuries ago. In the imperial census of 1795, however, in Tibet itself, which at the time was about the same size as today, there were only two million Tibetans.

In the census of 1953, 2,800,000 Tibetans were counted throughout all of China, of whom slightly more than 1,800,000 were outside Tibet proper, and slightly less than one million within Tibet itself.[17]

But meanwhile the Chamdo region of Tibet had been detached from Tibet in the last years of the Manchu dynasty, and arbitrarily turned into a new province, called Sikang province, which also contained the Khan (Kantze) district, now in Szechuan province. The reason for this will be dealt with in the next chapter, for it had to do with the British and their presence in Tibet. However, in 1955, the People's Government of China restored the Chamdo area to Tibet and abolished Sikang province, upon the demand of the Dalai Lama, formulated to Mao Tsetung in 1954. This added around 300,000 Tibetans living in the Chamdo region (also very depopulated, since the social system functioning there was the Tibetan one). Thus, by 1959, the population of Tibet was counted as 1,200,000. This still left 1,500,000 Tibetans outside Tibet, in the five other provinces of China.

'It seems the swiftest decline occurred after the reforms of Tsong Kapa,' writes Winnington.[18] 'For some 500 years, every day has drawn more men from the processes of production and reproduction.' Records of the population of one town, Bomi, compiled by order of the Manchu dynasty gave 30,000 as the population (early 1900s). By 1957, however, it was no more than 10,000.

The reasons for this decline were epidemics, poverty, the lamaist refusal to have any medical care introduced, and celibacy.

20 to 25 per cent of the male population was in monasteries, of which there were 2,711 in Tibet proper (excluding the five other provinces, but including Chamdo region).[19] In these there were 120,000 monks, and 13,000 nuns. If we estimate that in a population of roughly 1,200,000, 600,000 are male, this gives us one-fifth, or 20 per cent of all males as celibate monks. The figure does not include the 'children-lamas', aged between seven and fifteen, placed in monasteries by their parents through poverty. Such children were to be counted by the hundreds in the large monasteries.

The Tibetan people were deprived of adequate medical care and epidemics swept through the population, particularly smallpox.[20] Until 1949, the remedy for this was to dislodge the afflicted families, removing them to a far mountain, where they died of hunger or became the prey of wild beasts. Then there was also venereal disease, rampant even in the monasteries, with a very high rate of gonorrhoea, due to the social customs, causing sterility.[21] Add to this the high infant mortality rate, around 450 per thousand in the first year of life, due to lack of hygiene, and the fact that women gave birth in stables and cow-byres; last but not least, the enormous exploitation imposed upon the people by the 'three great masters', leading to the most wretched poverty.

Let us note, also, that such a 'genocide' — for that is what it is — also occurred among the Mongols, and for the same reasons: lamaism.

Thus the lack of people in this vast region today.

Corollary to the fear of the theocracy that any change would be detrimental to them, was the lack of good roads, and of wheeled vehicles. It was often said that the only wheel that turned in Tibet was the prayer wheel, and that all other wheels were forbidden. This is not quite true. One does find, in early 1950, that there were some motorcycles and even a few cars — all of them belonging to nobles or to high prelates — in Lhasa. But these vehicles had been brought over the mountain passes, on the backs of men, from India, piece by piece, and then re-assembled. Vast hordes of porters, thin, emaciated men and women, crawling up the steep mountain passes, were, with yaks and mules, the means of transport. Thus was brick tea carried, on the backs of men, in 400 lb. loads. This extremely costly, almost ruinous, method of transport was also an imposition upon the people. For everything had to be thus carried: the grain and firewood to the monasteries, by the serfs — peasants — as part of their *ula* or compulsory service, which was exactly the same as the medieval *corvée*. The supply of animals for transport also devolved upon the people, as did all other services for the 'three great masters'.

Around Lhasa itself, there were a couple of miles of fair road, upon which the motorcycles did run. It was not before the PLA arrived and the motorable roads were built that trucks and lorries began to appear, to the great resentment of the priestly order.

Since no industry was allowed, no coal mines — although coal is abundant in Tibet — were opened. The only fuel was wood, and for the poor, dried cow manure in round pats. Each noble house kept a large garden planted with fine trees to collect wood; but this was insufficient for the monasteries. Therefore another army of woodcutters and wood carriers was required. The most common view in photographs of Tibet before 1950 was, again, long files of men and women carrying firewood up the steps of monasteries and the Potala, to feed the charcoal braziers of the wealthy prelates. After 1950, coal mines were opened, and a search for oil instituted. For transport is impossible without fuel. Reafforestation in the Lhasa valley was also begun.

Thus the imperishable order of things in Tibet produced suffering, misery, and another 100 years of it would have caused extinction. Now all was to be changed. But the situation created by the theocracy was not propitious for change. How would the Chinese Revolution, when it reached Tibet, deal with 'the three lacks and the three abundances'?

2

Lhasa Only Yesterday

For centuries Lhasa was Jerusalem, Lourdes, Rome, Mecca, for believers in lamaism; the lodestone for millions of pilgrims from a vast area of Asia; from Mongolia in the north, from the five provinces of China where there are Tibetans, from Nepal, Kashmir, Bhutan and Sikkim; the Himalayan foothills on the Indian side, altogether far more numerous than the inhabitants of Tibet itself.[1] Their fervour was uncompromising, their minds oriented towards future reincarnation. Suffering and misery in this one was but the retribution of past sinfulness, and a pilgrimage to Lhasa would guarantee rebirth to a better life. Many sold all they had and came here, pouring prayer and gold and jewels and silk in supplication into the many temples and sanctuaries of the Holy City.

'In the town ... all is excitement, and noise, and pushing, and competition, every single soul ... being ardently occupied in the grand business of buying and selling. Commerce and devotion incessantly attract an infinite number of strangers ... the streets, always crowded ... a marvellous variety of physiognomies, costumes and languages. This immense multitude is for the most part transitory ... ' Thus Huc in 1846.[2]

'A tapestry of seventh-century life in medieval Europe ... monks, officials, nomads and peasants in a bustle of buying, selling, praying, begging and prostrating ... ' Thus Winnington in 1957.[3]

Lhasa was an immense caravanserai, and also a fantastic parasite. The Potala was Lhasa and Lhasa was the Potala. The town itself was small; in 1925 it was reckoned to hold no more

than 10,000 fixed inhabitants. Everywhere spread tents housing
the multitude of pilgrims. Lhasa was built in the days before
sanitation, and no house owned a latrine. People relieved
themselves anywhere, in the courtyards of houses, on the
streets, in the narrow lanes. Quite unselfconsciously, they
would squat when the urge took them. This was still the
custom in 1962. Since no toilet paper existed, the propagation
of intestinal disease (and of parasites, due to the consumption of
partly raw meat, even in the monasteries, as Patterson relates)[4]
was prevalent.

F. Spencer Chapman, secretary with the British Mission to
Lhasa in 1936, and author of *Lhasa Holy City*[5] found beggars
everywhere, 'some diseased and decrepit ... others able-bodied
and clamorous, needing nothing so much as a good whipping'(!)

Chapman described monks as 'unwashed insolent parasites',
'never have I seen a more evil-looking crowd'.

Perceval Landon, author of *Lhasa*,[6] found Buddhism in Tibet
bore not the faintest resemblance to the creed of Buddha. The
monks, he wrote, 'spare no effort to establish their predomi-
nance ... by fostering the slavish terror which is the whole
attitude to religion of the ignorant classes of the land.'

Even George N. Patterson, a confirmed pro-Dalai Lama
missionary, enormously hostile to present-day China, would
in his books complain of the lama system and especially of the
dogs afflicted with hydrophobia.

Dogs recur in almost every account of Tibet. Père Huc
speaks of 'the itch, leprosy ... and hydrophobic multitudes of
dogs', in 1846.[7] Patterson gives us an anecdote of a little girl
being bitten by a mad dog, and left to die, with the monks
refusing to give any medical care, since this was her destiny.
Dogs could not be killed, since killing was against the principles of the Buddhist religion. In 1955, Winnington wrote:
'Open heaps of rubbish – which are traditionally cleared once
a year – lie along some streets, a mixture of rotting substances
from which the purple-green carcass of a decomposing dog
juts out. Dogs are everywhere, ownerless dogs ... all night long

they bark and howl … band together and attack people so that it is quite dangerous to go on foot after dark.'[8]

The old city of Lhasa, a few hundred yards from the guest-house, has not changed its architecture, but of course the dogs, the beggars, the vermin, are gone. Every house is also a shop, sombre inside, and every house has a courtyard, with a well for water. But today the courtyards are no longer toilets, as they were; contamination proximate to the supply of water for drinking. Although in 1962 Stuart Gelder still found an 'overwhelming impression of dirt and squalor … no domestic drainage system and no arrangement for the disposal of sewage … ',[9] the dogs had disappeared, except for 'hundreds of charming pet dogs'. In 1975 this was changed, with the institution of inconspicuous public latrines and a system of removal (by night, not to offend). Lhasa is, as Gelder noted in 1962 'duller'. For today it is no longer a parasite–city, living on pilgrims. No longer do lords and ladies and high priests and government officials in splendid clothes ride through the streets followed by their retinues. But the streets are no longer public conveniences.

Today, new Lhasa is growing, and the old city is diminishing in size. I saw a bulldozer destroying some houses, which will be rebuilt with modern conveniences.[10] The whole structure upon which old Lhasa lived has gone, and the shops, which were of craftsmen turning out objects of religious worship, sculptures, jewellery, and leather goods, have become coopera-tives, still functioning, but directed towards consumption by the people themselves, or for export – Tibet is exporting goods even at the Canton fairs.[11]

What remains of old Lhasa then? Besides the old city, which is small,[12] there are the temples and sanctuaries, and the Potala. None of these, despite reports to the contrary, has been de-stroyed; but it would be mendacious to say that their function has not changed.

The complexion of the streets has changed. Gone are the caravans of yaks which in 1957 Winnington still saw producing a traffic jam with new convoys of lorries and trucks. Gone are the beggars, the monks, the dogs, the wood carriers, the pilgrims and their colourful and exotic hordes, light-hearted carriers of disease.

Gone the bustle. Gone the piles of rubbish, the hovels made of variegated garbage in which slaves and beggars huddled.

But the Jokka Kang, temple of temples, holiest and most sacred spot, still glows in the heart of the old city. And other sanctuaries and shrines, as far as I could make out, are also kept, placed under the care of the committee for the upkeep and restoration of monasteries, temples, and sanctuaries (composed of a conglomerate of ex-lamas, and Han Chinese).

I visited the Jokka Kang, 1,300 years old, built in A.D. 652 to commemorate the arrival of Princess Wen Cheng, and to house the Buddha statue she brought from China as a gift to her husband Songtsang Kampo and to his people. Upon this spot, so legend has it, a miraculous spring of water welled at her arrival ...

The approach to the Jokka Kang is through the circular, and once busiest shopping street of the old city, the Parkor, erstwhile regularly paced clockwise by pilgrims to attain merit. It is still a street lined with graceful mansions, and the Jokka Kang itself, in the past smothered from view, is now visible, its exterior walls and windows and painted galleries shielded from the sun by great curtains of black yak-wool. It is not of imposing dimensions. The marvellous carmine gate, with gold inscriptions in Tibetan, is not monumental, but it leads into a courtyard and then all is enchantment. The whole structure is a box within a box within a box, and the holiest and oldest of all is of course at its core. This is the original seventh-century structure, built to house the great Buddha Wen Cheng brought, and also to commemorate the joyful event of her coming. It was built by Chinese architects with Tibetan workmen, enlarged eight times, the last structure dating back to 1660.

The entrance, through a stone-flagged courtyard, sparkles

like a mirror with the body oil of innumerable pilgrims who prostrated themselves here. The whole structure is three-storeyed, and from the flat roof (with a slight incline to let the occasional rain drain out) protrude the gold-covered, copper canopies of shrines and sanctuaries housed within; this is common to all Tibetan temples and sanctuaries. The Jokka Kang was built and rebuilt during these 1,300 years, and the asymmetry of its graceful, red-pillared galleries and the clustered roofs of its terraced top, the way in which its thick interior walls are scooped out to provide niches and chapels in which statues are ensconced, add to its fascination. On the walls of the galleries frescoes of infernoes and heavens, deities, monsters and devils, cover every inch; one depicts the arrival of Princess Wen Cheng in Tibet, and the building of Lhasa upon the holy spring which then appeared. A well in the courtyard remains its evidence. There is indeed much easily accessible water below Lhasa. The frescoes are not only intact, but some appear to have been very carefully retouched, and others much older, were discovered when the dirt was removed. Landon[13] had observed that the 'paintings on the wall were barely distinguishable through a heavy coat of dirt and grease'. Winnington in 1955 found there was no ventilation in the smoke-dimmed interior, redolent of the smell of butter lamps, for every corridor was lined with lamps with slabs of butter in each chalice, every chapel coated with oily smoke, wafting 'a smell compounded of rancid butter, yak-dung smoke, incense, people and mustiness'. The Jokka Kang alone burnt 4,000 lbs of butter daily,[14] and this was not exceptional. Fully one-third of all the butter produced in Tibet went up in smoke in the near 3,000 temples, not counting the small altars in each house.

But now the building blazes with clean colour; the carved capitals above each pillar have been repainted and animals, birds and flowers glow in gold and turquoise, red and green and blue. The heavy steel curtains, closed with great steel padlocks before the main chapels, have been removed, save for one, in front of the most sacred statue of all, the Buddha brought by Wen Cheng so many centuries ago.

This chapel is so small that the statue fills it, so that a photograph of it whole is impossible. The statue, which is two metres high, sits on a silver-gilt throne flanked by pillars of solid silver, a canopy supported by silver dragons above its head. On its head is a thick gold crown with turquoises and small buddhas carved in gold; and behind it a great gold aura encrusted with precious stones. Around its breast are gold necklaces with marvellous pearls, turquoises and corals; its body is wrapped in rich brocade, embroidered with gold thread. All the walls are crowded with ex-votos, and smaller statues of pure gold and silver. Before the Buddha are lamps of solid gold and bowls of gold. The gold face is serene, with blue-lidded eyes; it looked down upon us, impassive, timeless.

The inner 'box' has pillars of stone, and now they have been cleaned they reveal frescoes of the Tang period, carved capitals and roof pillars with apsaras, a boon for archaeological study of the seventh century. There are dozens of other chapels, with large statues, and rows of smaller ones; corridors lined with devotional statues of guardians, living Buddhas, and other personalia of Buddhist lore. In the dimness they gesture with graceful hands, and the lamplight makes their painted faces with elongated eyes and their gesturing arms come alive. Here are the effigies of King Songtsang Kampo and his two wives, the Nepalese and the Chinese, arrayed in rich robes, life size, and lifelike. Behind the chapel where they are housed is a corridor leading to rooms where the few monks still living at the Jokka Kang stay.[15]

On the upper gallery is a reception room, carpeted, with lacquered gold and vermilion furniture, and square stools covered in satin which Tibetans sit upon. There I drank my first buttered tea, served by the keeper of the Jokka Kang, a Tibetan who had been a lama, but is now some sort of a curator. For it is obvious that the Jokka Kang is no longer a place of worship; no crowd is here, and except for some incense burning in front of some of the statues, I only noticed one old woman, who seemed to be doing some praying.

In the stone courtyard, sheltered from the sun by a yak-wool awning, stood the dreaded female guardian of the Dalai Lama, the goddess Palden Lhamo. She had previously been on the top gallery but 'we have demoted her' said the keeper, indicating that evil must not be placed above such holy figures as the Great Buddha, or King Songtsang Kampo's likeness. Palden Lhamo is the Tibetan counterpart of the goddess Durga of Hindu mythology; she rides a mule, eats the warm brains from a human skull in her hand, and has chaplets and necklaces of human skulls about her. She has a marvellously cruel face, and her robes are sewn with pearls and rubies.

We climbed on to the very top of the Jokka Kang and under the dazzling sun its various roofs were a blaze of gold; with dragons' heads and bells and birds and deer, all of copper-covered gold. They framed, as if by design, a view of the hills with the Potala.

For all its beauty, the Jokka Kang was also an engine of oppression and lama rapacity; no entrance could be effected before tribute was paid; each chapel also had its tribute. Here, as elsewhere, the monks levied their own religious taxes upon the people, and each of its 2,000 images and statuettes was a tax-gatherer.

Out into the street, where now a crowd had gathered. Surrounded by a small wall is the pillar set up to commemorate the advent of Tang law, and a willow reputedly planted by Princess Wen Cheng. The air smelt sweet and I looked up to the incredible indigo sky and found all the flat roofs of the surrounding houses peopled with grown-ups and children, looking down at me. I also noticed a loudspeaker at an angle of the temple building. The houses, meticulously whitewashed, had painted windowsills and frames and overhangs, and painted door lintels; at each window flowered not only geraniums but also eager, smiling faces. Good-naturedly the crowd cheered, children ran up to shake hands. I wondered whether, among

the older ones there, some perhaps missed the past? Perhaps
as one misses carnival, a feast. On the other hand, this past was
a monster devouring their lives. I would have to find out
whether a new ethic, a new logic of the world, was beginning
to replace this world of sumptuous terror where statues were
so extravagantly bejewelled.

The Jokka Kang had taken a whole afternoon. A long morning
had to be given to visit the Potala. My hosts were not sure I
could do it; they recalled that 'some people cannot climb
before a week or two'. It is only another 300 metres or so up,
but taxing at Lhasa's altitude. And there are no lifts.

My Shanghai sedan drove only half the way up by the back
road, for the front of the Potala is inaccessible by car; the hill-
slope entirely occupied by the enormous 125-step stone staircase which goes right down to city level, and by a collection of
Tibetan houses, formerly the houses of employees of the various
'ministries' of the Dalai Lama's cabinet. One of them, a small
white structure, was pointed out to me as 'the justice court'.

'A Versailles, but vertical.' This was the verdict of a French
friend of mine, to whom I showed my pictures of the Dalai
Lama's former residence. It is, according to Winnington, 100
feet higher than the top of St Paul's cross. It measures 178
metres in height upon the 130-metre or so hill, and is 400
metres from east to west. As Versailles, the Potala is now a
museum.

Like the Jokka Kang, the Potala's inner core dates back to
the seventh century, and is at hilltop level. To understand the
hodge-podge of its inner structure, the best parallel is the
Bayon of Angkor, Cambodia, which also was restructured
from within during the centuries to add galleries, chambers,
sanctuaries; so that the marvellous outside symmetry gives no
idea of its interior maze. As a result, the Potala's thirteen
storeys must be climbed—I climbed them—by tortuous,
ladder-like wooden stairs, stuck in the corners of galleries and
rooms somewhat haphazardly. These alternate with stone

staircases, obviously built at an earlier time. There are half-flights leading at different levels into different galleries, and the whole honeycomb of one thousand rooms defies any rational description. To reach some of the large prayer halls, chapels, apartments, one has to squeeze behind pillars through invisible small doors that open out of painted walls, or slide behind enormous brocade curtains, themselves hidden behind huge carved screens, or push open what looks like a pair of window shutters flush with a gallery face and find it leads to a precipitous flight of steps hurtling into utter darkness ... Once upon a time all electric torches were forbidden in the Potala as malefic, and butter lamps were used everywhere. Now there is electric light. The few solitary bulbs which hang in the large rooms struggle valiantly, but fail, to light the stairs. One simply gropes on, even with an electric torch.

Within the Potala is a chapel scooped out in sheer rock; there on a ledge are the statues of King Songtsang Kampo, and three, not two wives, the Tibetan one holding a child in her arms, and placed by the bronze cooking pot of the royal family. The King's face is, as in the Jokka Kang, handsome and energetic, with a gallant small moustache; the Nepalese wife is certainly the most beautiful, and Wen Cheng has a charming, gentle smile. As for the Tibetan one, she is more fleshy, and plain, but the child in her arms is strikingly like his father, bar the moustache.

It was King Songtsang Kampo who began the Potala, known then as the Red Palace. The name Potala, which means Buddha's mountain, came later; though Lhasa's name, which means City of the Sun, was already in use in the eighth century. The Potala was destroyed and rebuilt several times; only a chapel of Kuanyin, housing also the effigies of the King and his wives, remains from the original. The present structure dates to A.D. 1642 when the Great Fifth became the absolute ruler of Tibet and moved here from the Drepung monastery. It took fifty years to build the Potala we see today, and many thousands of slaves. There are 1,000 rooms, 10,000 chapels, and

around 200,000 statues, statuettes of all sizes. It has six large
gates, and two round defence towers east and west. It contains
the tombs housing the bodies, wrapped in clay and then
covered in gold leaf, of six Dalai Lamas, all except, of course,
the gay poet, the Sixth, and those who died mysteriously in
adolescence.

In this termite nest, all the galleries are painted, as are all the
rooms; or decorated with rows upon rows of golden statuettes;
everywhere hang, enveloping the pillars, rich brocades; ceil-
ings of the main chanting rooms and prayer rooms are draped
in silk, and there are carpets—some of them priceless, others
obviously imported and, curiously, of British make—covering
the floors.

Adequate description is shallow, for after some hours of
padding behind guides, up and down, round and round, in and
out, one's mind is out of breath, even if one's feet continue
walking. The exterior magnificence is easier to describe, and
also to photograph: a height enhanced by walls which slope
inward from their base so that it appears to grow from its
mountain pedestal and to continue it; brilliant, whitewashed
walls with a deep crimson middle structure sited upon a level
terrace; its several roofs and canopies all gold-covered; the
receding windows, narrower at top than bottom (as in all the
mansions in old Lhasa), creating the optical illusion of further
height; the large stone stairway, broad enough for several
horsemen to ride abreast, which crosses the front façade from
south to north-west, turns sharply north-east and then north-
west once more, in a tremendous zigzag; the lake and water
meadows, a paradise of cool water and green leaves, which
form the park at the back, the small pavilion built by the
romantic Sixth at the water's edge ...

Of the tombs of previous Dalais, the most imposing are the
Thirteenth and the Fifth. The Fifth's tomb is sixty feet high, but
the Thirteenth's is seventy feet; both rise, within the interior
of the Potala, through three storeys, so that their tops are level
with a gallery two floors higher than the tomb's base. The

thirteenth Dalai's spectacular sepulchre is covered in gold; some 18,800 ounces of it over its solid silver base and the bulbous middle section which houses the body. The tomb of the Great Fifth is also gold-covered, only slightly more modest. The bases rest in large rooms filled with a profusion of personal possessions, and gifts of all kinds: there are jade cups, porcelain vases, a belt studded with 200,000 small pearls. The cone which rises from the spherical body of the tomb is surmounted by a bell on which the rising sun and moon are engraved; and the whole surface of these structures is studded with precious stones: turquoise, amethyst, coral, sapphires, lapis lazuli, diamonds and rubies.

The throne room is also amazing, with its silk-covered ceiling, painted walls, carpets, hangings, and the great throne covered in heavy crimson brocade. It is in this throne room that, in 1904, the British expedition under Colonel Younghusband, after storming Lhasa, forced the signature of a convention upon the council of ministers of the Dalai Lama (the latter had fled to China to escape capture by the British).[16]

The Dalai Lama's private apartments are in the crimson middle palace, a winter residence where he lived from November to March. The rooms are small, and at the very top of the Potala, entirely swathed in silk and brocade and carpets. The small carved bed is set against walls covered with Tantric paintings, but in another room one finds an English iron bed, such as are used in boarding schools, and which is ordinary length ... perhaps the Dalai Lama was tired of having to sit up, in the Buddha position, all night. The toilet is a hole in the ground; droppings went plumb down 400 feet. Tibetans have assured me that it was quite true they were piously stored to pound into medicinal pills, although other reports deny that it was so. The toilet seat, a small aperture in a slab of wood, is lined with pale pink velvet.

Another section of the Potala labyrinth is the white palace, built after 1910 by the thirteenth Dalai Lama. Its walls are also covered with paintings, and among them are figures of the period, including the Chinese Empress Dowager, and the British Prince of Wales.

But no single storey is continuous throughout the whole structure. One is always climbing or descending steps. At last one gets on to the terrace roof; and there protrude the marvellous gold-covered canopies of the tombs below, adorned with jutting dragons and other symbols; and large bell-like cones, with gold lettering of the Holy Writ. Here also is the sanctuary where the edicts of the Chinese emperor Chien Lung are kept.

Statues, statues, and objects, objects; some shoddy, others priceless; artificial paper flowers, cheap clocks, cheap vases, a rather horrible tea set—it appears that the Dalai Lama took tea 'English fashion'. 'He had had an English tutor for a while ... the whole family was much influenced because they often went to Calcutta to purchase many things.' This appears to be correct. I had heard about these shopping trips in India. Mules or horses loaded with solid gold ingots provided the money for the expenses of the Dalai Lama's family. In the main throne room a chandelier with electric bulbs, of dubious taste, hung right before the Dalai Lama's throne. A present, it is said, from the British Mission to Lhasa in 1936.

And then, among that enormous heap of things, things, things, I noticed here and there bowls made of human skulls, and human thigh bones, with delicate silver handles. Apparently these were also in use; but the curators both Tibetan (a woman and a man) were unwilling or unable to explain them exactly. As for the Han Chinese, they observe towards customs they repudiate a tactful silence, at least in Tibet itself.

The Potala, classified a national treasure, is scrupulously clean, whereas it was not so before. The number of people employed in feeding its inhabitants and bringing all that was needed must have been considerable. The main staircase, said my hosts, saw a constant flow of porters carrying firewood and butter, as well as a horde of noblemen and prelates. Below the Potala, thousands of pilgrims knelt in adoration; they would never see the face of the God-King; for on his rare excursions he was in a palanquin, and behind hangings, while strong-arm and burly guards armed with long sticks beat back the crowds on his passage.

Out of the Potala, and down the hill among the scramble of buildings on its southern slope, to inspect the justice court with its two red pillars; here religious offenders were tied to be beaten. The gouging of eyes and maiming of hands and feet, which were customary punishment – as in medieval Europe – for offences by the serfs and the slaves, were also practised here.[17] 'In the early years we often heard the howls and screams ... and we saw people on the streets with the cangue, or with irons on their feet ... but we could do nothing, because we could not interfere,' said the Han Chinese to me. 'Reforms of any kind could only begin after the Dalai Lama went away.'

At the bottom of the Potala hill are the dungeons; a hole in the ground. Into this prisoners were thrown, especially debtors; their families had to come to feed them. 'There were scorpions and other vermin in that hole,' exclaimed Madame Chen, her voice quivering with prolonged indignation. 'When the Dalai Lama left, we took out the people who were in it ... one was a child two days old. His mother had been flung into the hole, and had given birth there.'

As we left the Potala I turned back to look at it; lodestone and magnet for so many, so many centuries, it stood now, aloof, in splendid isolation. Now I had seen its inside, I could no longer feel entranced as I gazed upon its marvellous beauty. It was an evil, parasitic monster, despite the glamour and the romance with which it had been invested for so long.

The next day was occupied by a visit to the Norbulingka, the summer palace of the Dalai Lama, where he resided from March to October every year. It is about 4 kilometres from the Potala, and on flat ground. The name means Jewel Park. A much smaller palace, it stands in a very large, fine garden, which covers round 100 acres, full of trees and flowers, and with a small stream in the middle, spanned by marble bridges and reflecting graceful, cool pavilions. Unlike the Potala, it has no definite architecture, but seems a mix-up of several; and the main gate is quite absurdly comic: two white and green lions, with slavering red tongues, of atrocious taste, flank it. They were a present from the late Manchu dynasty, or from Chiang Kai-shek; no one could remember exactly ...

According to the Dalai Lama in 1959 the Norbulingka had been shelled and left a smoking ruin by the Chinese Army. I had already ascertained that the Potala and the Jokka Kang were not damaged.[18] The Norbulingka was also left intact. 'We have looked after everything and we have left everything just as it was when the Dalai Lama rose from his bed here in the early morning of March 17, 1959, and left,' said the keepers — one Han, one Tibetan — to me.

The Norbulingka gardens are now a public park and on Sundays and holidays the people come here in families, to picnic (the Tibetans love picnics), to sing and to dance under the trees, among the flower beds filled with dahlias and chrysanthemums.

The Norbulingka consists of several buildings, pavilions and palaces. I saw them all. Building started in 1755, and it is the biggest garden in Tibet. But because of the use of butter lamps everywhere — in the Potala, some of them took half a hundred-weight of butter at a time, but here, they seem to have been smaller — fires were common. The new Norbulingka or Chensel Phodrang was rebuilt only in 1954 to 1956; to rebuild it, vast amounts of gold and jewellery were collected from believers; who also sent the Dalai Lama a magnificent gold-covered throne.

Within the apartments of the Dalai Lama, the same splendour leavened with bad taste; statues, statues; extraordinary carpets, magnificent hangings; and some tawdry stuff too. Painted walls, some of them showing episodes of the Dalai Lama's life.

In the Dalai Lama's bedroom, no longer are butter lamps

kept burning, to await his return.[19] But the bed, from which he
rose on that fateful March dawn is still kept exactly as he left it.
There is a yellow brocade coverlet, its end turned up, as if it
had just been pushed away; I lifted the mattress and found
mothballs, put there to preserve it. 'We want to show that all
is left as it was, nothing is changed.' None of the habitations of
the previous incarnations, which dot the park, have been
changed either.

'Would you think the Dalai Lama is likely to return?' I asked,
as we took buttered tea in the reception room. 'We do not
know,' was the answer. And, later, it seemed so pointless to
ask it.

In this palace, objects from the late Manchu dynasty—the
Ch'ing—are very much in evidence. The atmosphere of the
inner apartments is one of more relaxed, daily living. There
is a modern w.c., and a bathroom, but with no pipes attached.[20]
And there are Thermos flasks in the bathroom. The garden is
sheer delight, gentle deer walk about, being the animals con-
nected with Buddha's life story. One of them followed me
right up to the gate, but when I wanted to photograph it it
suddenly ran back into the trees.

British influence, too, is here. In the clock, made in Birming-
ham (of all places). Some of the table lamps, some carpets
(Axminster), and the crockery. Perhaps the assertion that the
Dalai Lama 'and some of the three great masters round him
had an English way of life' is not altogether convincing. The
mere fact of taking yak butter, or milk, in tea, is not proof of
British influence.

However, that evening, at the guesthouse, we discussed
again Tibet's past, Lhasa's past. There had been, once again, a
frontier clash between India and China.[21] It was minor, and
the Chinese treated it as such; so did the Indians. But it brought
to mind again the question of national boundaries, and of the
insurrection which had taken place in 1959, and changed Tibet
so much.

The root of all these events lay in history, and in Tibet's past

4

history, Great Britain too had had a share; which perhaps also explains why some people in England still cling to the illusion that 'China invaded Tibet'.

British interest in Tibet was a corollary of its conquest of India and maintenance of its rule there. In Bhutan and Sikkim, the people were also Tibetan in religion and customs, and these states were tributaries of Tibet. In 1770 the British advanced into Sikkim and the Panchen Lama asked them to stop. In 1774 Bogle was the first Englishman to visit Tibet. He went to Shigatze, seat of the Panchen Lama, to try to conclude a trade agreement. His proposals were referred to the Chinese imperial court in Peking, since the local authorities had no power to make such agreements. Bogle, and his colleague Captain Turner, reported on the immense wealth of the land; gold and musk and borax, skin and turquoises. Gold especially, simply washed out of every stream. They also noted the vast quantities of tea consumed by the Tibetans in their thrice-daily tsampa. The next century saw steady attempts to wrest the tea trade away from China for the benefit of tea plantations in North Assam and in Darjeeling.

Control of Sikkim provided the best route to Tibet, and the Sikkimese were pressured into building such a road to Tibet for the British. Colonel Austin Waddell, in his book, *Lhasa and its Mysteries*,[22] tells of the use of spies by the British, in order to get maps of Tibet. They employed for the most part Tibetans settled on the Indian side of the Himalayas, trained them to plot out routes and to make maps. These men pretended to be pilgrims, and concealed long strips of paper for recording compass bearings in their prayer wheels. 'To escape detection was wellnigh impossible for a European.' Père Huc also tells, in his book, of one Moorcroft, an Englishman who went to Lhasa from Ladakh in Kashmir, and was successful in passing himself off as a Kashmiri; and Kashmiri merchants were often to be seen in Lhasa.[23]

In 1890 Sikkim was detached from Tibet by the British, who

then pressured the Chinese court into signing a treaty recognizing a new border, and the loss of Sikkim. At the time China was weakened by the Opium Wars and torn by internal strife; the Manchu court was pusillanimous, and though the local Tibetan hierarchy was indignant and clamoured for a Chinese army to be sent to the rescue — as had been done before — none was sent. In 1893 a trade treaty provided for duty-free imports from India into Tibet, with a Chinese customs house under British 'supervision' — which then meant control.

By then British preoccupation with the Russian Czarist advance into Asia was intense. Russia had now reached the Pamirs; and Russian agents were, supposedly, everywhere; in India, 'making trouble', and also in Persia and Afghanistan. The north-west frontier of the Indian subcontinent became a major problem of defence against the Russian Empire. British policy was to organize Persia, Afghanistan, and Tibet into buffer states, but with dominant British influence, against Russian advance. In 1902 it was rumoured that the Russians had an agent in Lhasa, a Buryat-Mongol lama, called Dorjieff, who was studying at the Drepung monastery, the largest monastery in Tibet and also in the world.

Whether Dorjieff was an agent or not is not proved; but the British now intervened. In December 1903 a British expeditionary force, under Colonel Francis Younghusband and Brigadier J. R. MacDonald, invaded Tibet via Yatung and Gyantze. The time was well chosen, since the Russians were then involved in war with the Japanese, and China was prostrate after the harsh indemnities and the humiliations inflicted upon her to punish the Chinese people after the Boxer Uprising.

In August 1904 Younghusband reached Lhasa, killing 1,500 men of the small Tibetan army, which was ill-trained and ill-equipped.[24] The Dalai Lama fled to Peking for protection, and in the Potala's throne room the British forced the chief minister and the head pontiffs of Lhasa's three main monasteries, Sera, Gaden, and Drepung, to sign a convention giving up Sikkim, providing for the opening of trade markets, and making Tibet a British sphere of influence. 'Without the consent of Great Britain no foreign power shall be permitted to send either official or non-official persons to Tibet, no matter in what pursuit they may be engaged ... or to construct roads or railways or erect telegraphs or open mines ... '

However, the convention specified that China was not to be considered 'a foreign power', and this was ratified in a further convention in 1906, signed in Peking, by which China's sovereign rights in Tibet were recognized. By then, however, a subtle play on words occurred, the word *suzerainty* instead of *sovereignty* being used; this would five decades or more later be picked up by Mr Nehru, when independent India inherited, along with the partition created by British imperial policy, also some inclination to continue clinging on to what had been acquired through pressure and force. China paid an indemnity of £500,000 sterling to the British for the aggression practised by the latter upon Tibet. And the Dalai Lama, who had fled to avoid capture by the British, returned under Chinese escort to Lhasa.

In 1907 a further secret agreement between Great Britain and Russia relating to Persia, Afghanistan and Tibet was signed in St Petersburg. Both states recognized 'the suzerain rights of China in Tibet' and engaged 'not to enter into negotiations with Tibet except through the intermediary of the Chinese government'.

But in 1909, with uprisings all over China due to the incipient first Chinese Revolution (of 1911) a Chinese general, Chao Erh-feng, marched into the Chamdo area of Tibet, and to 'pacify' the region, cut off the Chamdo area from Tibet, incorporating it into a new province, called Sikang province.[25] This aroused the fury of the Tibetans, and the depredations committed by the Chinese troops also left much bitterness behind. The thirteenth Dalai Lama now turned to Britain and fled to India. He found, however, that the British were intent on annexing Tibet, under cover of 'independence'. Under pressure, such a declaration was made, but soon after the Chinese Revolution of 1911 occurred, and the Dalai Lama returned to Lhasa. A conference was called at Simla, in 1913, between representatives of the Chinese government, Tibet, and Great Britain.

Now entered on the scene Sir Charles Bell; since 1908 he had been patiently cultivating nobles in the entourage of the Dalai Lama; and at the conference he pressed for an agreement splitting Tibet.[26] This was regarded by the Dalai Lama as an act of treachery, and was also repudiated by the Chinese government. However, while the conference was proceeding, a 'forward policy' was adopted by the British. A much longer section of the boundary between Tibet and British India was now altered. This was the so-called MacMahon Line. Drawn up in March 1914, it wrested from Tibet 90,000 square kilometres of territory, which are now known as NEFA (North East Frontier Administration) and which present-day India has incorporated.

'Until 1910,' writes Alistair Lamb,[27] 'the government of British India considered that its international boundary eastwards of Bhutan ran along the foot of the Himalayan range on the northern side of the Brahmaputra valley. By 1914 it had been decided to move the line northwards ... '

'The validity of this transaction', he continues, 'is certainly open to question, and the Chinese have consistently, in both Kuomintang and Maoist times, refused to be bound by it.'

The British at the Simla conference of 1914 claimed the signatures of both Tibetan and Chinese representatives; but the Chinese government repudiated the latter—his name, funnily enough, was Ivan Ho! And the Tibetan 'plenipotentiary' who signed was a minor local official, also later repudiated by Lhasa.[28]

While I was in Tibet in 1975, I had an interview with Tien Pao, a senior Tibetan official, who recalled the bitterness of the Tibetans at this loss of territory. 'We are the ones who feel most injured by the MacMahon line ... We hope that India, a great country and a great people, will sit down and negotiate, as equal to equal, the whole border between our region of Tibet and India, which has never been delimited by our two nations, China and India, as independent states.'

In the 1920s it was British policy to cultivate contacts with some of the 'three great masters' and to create a 'pro-British' group among the Tibetan nobles. After the First World War, an English school for the children of the nobility was set up in Gyantze[29] in 1921. But opposition was strong, especially from the lamas, who were terrified at the idea of such a school. Among the nobility, however, it was attractive. By then Tibetan nobles were beginning to send their sons to English schools in Kalimpong, Darjeeling, and other places in north India where there are also Tibetans. For education, except religious, was non-existent in Tibet itself. Thus a small nucleus of nobles who 'speak excellent English, sit for Senior Cambridge and go back to merchandising or their official sinecures' was being formed. This of course did not affect the serfs, artisans, slaves, for whom there had never been education of any sort.[30]

In 1926, due to religious opposition, the school had to close down. However, British influence did continue through the sending of missions to Tibet, notably the one in 1936 led by B. J. Gould, with Spencer Chapman as its secretary.

The British trained a certain number of Tibetan officers (all army officers were of noble families) in India for a Tibetan army, and so maintained a permanent mission in Lhasa, which was still there when the Chinese Revolution of 1949 occurred.[31] According to Bell,[31] it was no secret that Great Britain was to push through an arrangement by which she would not only supply arms and equipment to Tibet, but also provide mining prospectors; and extend a telegraph line from India to Lhasa. A geological mission, under the conduct of an Indian 'holy man' prospected for minerals in Tibet and the findings are recorded in the *Encyclopaedia Britannica*'s pages on Tibet.

But unrest simmered among the monasteries; for the

British were enlisting the help of a powerful layman, Tsarong, who was a *Kalon* or minister, commander-in-chief of the army and master of the mint as well. The lama order feared that Britain would try to restore a secular government.

Sir Charles Bell had noted that 'by 1925 the Dalai Lama (who was supposed to be pro-British) was turning strongly away ... towards China'. As for the Panchen Lama, he had fled to Tsinghai in 1923, fearful of his life because of his opposition to the pro-British policies of some of the nobles in Lhasa.

The attempts made by Spencer Chapman and the British Mission in 1936 to get the Panchen Lama to return failed. In 1939 war came to Europe, and after the Second World War, India's independence in 1947 would herald the swift decline of the British Empire. However, India's leaders would now inherit some of the thinking which had guided British foreign policy for so many decades. In 1950, when the main body of the British Mission to Lhasa left for India, one man, Richardson, was left behind, 'to suggest an element of permanency ... ' wrote Chapman. Left behind as well was a radio man, Robert Ford, who was in Chamdo when the PLA marched in and was arrested as a 'British agent' but subsequently released.

And yet, in 1945, Great Britain had taken the initiative of sending a letter to the Chinese government, restating that Tibet was part of China, and in 1943 the American State Department also sent a statement saying it did not challenge the Chinese assertion that 'the region of Tibet is part of China'. But by 1949, the Chinese Revolution had precipitated America into a policy of hostility by all possible means and methods, to 'Red China'.

It is at this moment that Lowell Thomas and his son, L. T. Jr, appeared on the scene. There were going to be renewed intrigues to try to detach Tibet from China. Lowell Thomas went to Lhasa and met Richardson. 'The most important requirement, of course, is skilful guerrilla forces,' wrote Lowell Thomas Jr, 'to create these, Tibet needs arms and advice, principally from outside.' And Richardson was invited to tour the USA giving lectures on Tibetan 'independence' from China. The statements of 1943 and 1945 were now forgotten.

Meanwhile a new Dalai Lama (the present one, fourteenth in succession, and born in 1935) and a new Panchen Lama (the tenth, born in 1936) had been found; they were, in 1950, youths of fifteen and fourteen.

Lowell Thomas and his son, equipped with electronic devices, arrived in Lhasa in August 1949. America was preparing to recognize Tibet as a sovereign state and to support Tibet's application for membership of the United Nations. The Thomases spent a week in Lhasa as the basis for a publicity campaign in favour of Tibetan independence.[32] Lowell Thomas Jr admitted that a Foreign Office report that radioactive minerals—the metal for the atom bomb—had been found in Tibet was also an inducement to these manœuvres.[33]

When the People's Liberation Armies advanced in 1950 into south and south-west China, declaring it would liberate the whole territory of China, the Dalai Lama and his family with some of the ministers, and a large retinue, fled to India. The Chinese, always mindful of his youth, never accused him of having been more than 'manipulated' into this. The Tibetan cabinet was divided, some favouring alliance with the new Chinese regime. When the PLA reached Chamdo (at the time not included in Tibet, but part of Sikang province) a battle took place between the PLA and Tibetan troops, under the command of Ngapo Nawang Jigme, a great nobleman and minister in the Dalai Lama's cabinet.[34]

The battle of Chamdo in October 1950 was a turning point.[35] Ngapo Nawang Jigme, called familiarly in Chinese, Apei, was defeated and captured. The Tibetans were won over by the extraordinary good behaviour of the Red armies. They only knew the warlord and the Kuomintang soldiers, no better than bandits. But these were Sajami, 'the new Hans'. They did not enter monasteries or places of worship, and above all, they helped the population, took 'not a needle or thread, not a single grain of barley', and their medical teams immediately set to healing the sick. 'We had been given much detailed instructions as to how to behave,' one of the army men told A. L. Strong.[36]

Ngapo Nawang Jigme, himself a patriot and a far-sighted man, now personally pleaded with the other ministers and the Dalai Lama for re-attachment to China, even communist, as the only means of salvation for Tibet. He became the main link between the new government and the Tibetan officials in Lhasa and also in Delhi. The PLA did not cross over into Tibet territory proper, awaiting the result of his negotiations.[37]

In Delhi the Dalai Lama's entourage now made a volte-face. They said that they had been on their way to Peking via Delhi, with the Dalai Lama, but that because of the civil war in China, it was easier to reach Peking via Delhi and Hongkong than through the footpaths out of Tibet, since all the roads in China were unsafe with looting Kuomintang deserters and bandits. The British authorities in Hongkong, however, refused to issue visas for the Tibetans to go through Hongkong to China. Ngapo Nawang Jigme urged the Dalai Lama to return to Lhasa, as otherwise Tibet would become a prey of 'imperialism'. And the Dalai Lama returned.

The newly independent government of India was aware of American and British intrigues in Tibet; and Nehru as a Socialist and an Asian did not wish, at the time, to be marked down as a tool of 'imperialism'.[38] On October 24 the PLA announced that it intended to continue its advance into Tibet proper, and four days later the Indian government broadcast the news that the Tibetan delegation had left Delhi on the 25th to return to Lhasa, and placed the onus for the delay in the Tibetan delegation's proceeding to Peking upon the British refusal to give visas via Hongkong.

October 1950 was a crucial month in Asia. Since the end of June 1950 the Korean war had been on; and it was in that October that Chinese volunteers went to North Korea. The

Indian government had good relations with the new government of the People's Republic, proclaimed on October 1, and was anxious not to damage them. However, even then Nehru raised the matter of privileges in Tibet inherited from the British colonial administration of India, and of previous treaties. 'The government of India are anxious that these establishments which do not detract in any way from Chinese *suzerainty* over Tibet ... should continue.'

The Chinese welcomed Nehru's assertions that India had 'no political or territorial ambitions in Tibet', but were obviously unwilling to agree to Nehru's demands to maintain, as the British had done, an agent of the Indian government in Lhasa, trade agencies, telegraphs and posts, and military escorts to 'protect the trade route' which the British had established at the Younghusband invasion. They reiterated the principles of peaceful co-existence and hoped that 'all problems of Sino-Indian diplomatic commercial and cultural relations in connection with Tibet can be solved ... ' But they made it clear they brooked no outside interference in what was an internal matter of China.

However, the ambiguity, and the frontier problem, were to persist, despite a trade agreement in 1954 in which the Indian government agreed that Tibet was part of China and withdrew the agent. This agreement was the prelude to Bandung; it provided the background of solidarity necessary for the impressive rise of the Third World which then began. Even in 1950, all maps of the boundaries between Tibet and India were already being 'overhauled' in India; and a comparison with the maps of the 1940s shows this clearly. Within the next decade, more than eighteen geographical publications, including British ones, would not be allowed into India because they did not show the boundaries 'correctly'. Even the map in Nehru's own book, his autobiography, published in England, did not correspond to the new maps brought out. A comparison between a British map and its 'boundaries', the Chinese, and the subsequent Indian overhauls, establishes this fact rather clearly.[39]

At long last, in April 1951, the Tibetan delegation with Ngapo Nawang Jigme as plenipotentiary arrived in Peking. Not only the Dalai Lama, but also the Panchen Lama, who had taken refuge in China once again, returned to Lhasa, and to Shigatze respectively. Three weeks later, on May 23, 1951, an agreement was signed, called the 17-point agreement. The PLA, who had not moved from Chamdo since October 1950, now entered Lhasa without a shot being fired, in September 1951, with a music band and a concourse of lamas from the monasteries blowing great silver conches in welcome.

3

Rifles in the Rice Heap — the Insurrection of 1959

The entry of the PLA into Lhasa at first changed nothing of the old theocratic order. The military presence was minimal; a garrison of 1,500 men. The main bulk of the army was busy building roads, the first from Chengtu to Lhasa was completed in 1954, almost an incredible feat, across fourteen of the world's highest mountain ranges and twelve big rivers. Every six to ten miles along it were strung repair and maintenance teams, petrol stores for the lorries and vehicles.[1] Along the roads the PLA established State farms on reclaimed land, producing its own food and rearing its own animals and fodder. For the whole region was not only scantily populated, but on a subsistence agriculture level; it could not support a large influx of people. The PLA was strictly enjoined not to take even a needle or thread from the people, an order they followed scrupulously, not interfering even when they felt revolted by the beatings or the maimings, which were the usual punishments for offenders.

But a road is not only a highway for rolling vehicles; it is also an instrument of change, and very early the great prelates, the pontiffs and the lords, seeing it built, must have felt that time was not on their side. The wheel was here, and it meant a great many things, including the fact that trade (which had been in the hands of noble families and merchant-lamas) would now also be altered.

Alterations were already signalled, in an understated way, in the 17-point agreement of May 23, 1951. 'The Tibetan nationality is one of the nationalities with a long history within the boundaries of China and, like many other nationalities, it has done its glorious duty in the course of the creation and development of the great mother land ... ' ran the preamble. It then stated that 'there would be national regional autonomy under the unified leadership of the Central Government', that the central authorities would not alter the existing political system in Tibet, and would recognize the established status and functions and powers of the Dalai and Panchen Lamas. Officials of various ranks would hold office as usual, there would be freedom of religious beliefs and the monasteries would be protected; the Tibetan troops would be reorganized into the PLA to become part of the national defence forces of China. *In matters related to various reforms in Tibet, there will be no compulsion ... the local government of Tibet should carry out reforms on its own accord ... '*

The Central Government was willing to give time for change, but change there must be. And change was already there, by the mere fact that, in building the road, the PLA also employed local Tibetans, who, for the first time in their lives, were not doing *corvée*, but being paid *wages* ... and *wages* were unknown in Tibet. The wages they received, the fair and kindly treatment they got, were already a revolution. 'High wages have encouraged even monks to doff their robes and go to work in borrowed homespun,' wrote Winnington.[2] 'The Hans worked side by side with us ... they did not whip us ... for the first time I was treated as a human being.'[3]

Then there were also the PLA medical teams. Everywhere the army went they found a total absence of medical care; the medical teams were soon busy curing sick children, men and women. This, also, was a great threat to religious authority.

And finally, there was the fact that Tibetans are sprawled over such a vast area of China. Already in the Tibetan districts of Szechuan, Kantze and Apa, the Revolution was expropriating big landlords and monasteries, and land reform was starting ... The same was taking place in Tsinghai province. By 1951 the abbot of Kumbum, brother of the Dalai

Lama, had fled to America. How could one half of the Tibetan population be liberated, and the other half remain serfs and slaves?

In the great monasteries opposition began, already as early as 1950. Then trouble broke out, as serfs revolted and were put down. To understand how all this climaxed in the flight of the Dalai Lama in 1959—a climax which was also the end of Old Tibet and the beginning of New Tibet—I visited one of the three great monasteries of the Lhasa valley, one which had been not only a powerful force in the theocracy, but also a hotbed of the insurrection: Drepung, or the Rice Heap.

The monasteries possessed 37 per cent of the cultivated land and pasture in Tibet; the aristocracy 25 per cent, and the remaining 38 per cent were in the hands of government officials as perquisites for holding posts in the government.[4] Freehold land to individual farmers was almost unheard of; everyone belonged to 'a master', and cultivated land held from 'a master'. It did happen that serfs ran away and became 'black people'—*duichuns*—to escape debt and being sold as slaves, and settled on unused land; but pretty soon they would again fall under a 'master' who could sell them, use their services, exact *corvée* (ula), forbid their marriage if it took them away from his property where it was their duty to labour for his benefit, and punish them at will.

Drepung is the largest monastery in the world. It is on the road westwards towards Shigatze, and about 12 kilometres from Lhasa. There one sees what looks like a white town in a pocket of hills. Hence its name, the Rice Heap (Drepung). Merely to whitewash the whole of it once a year (a custom in Lhasa) must have taken thousands of people, working for nothing but a pittance.

Drepung, like all monasteries, owned serfs. It had 185 manorial estates with a population of 25,000 serfs, and 300 pastures with 16,000 herdsmen; or a total of 40,000 people who toiled for it. It had special privileges, and the right to levy taxes (all monasteries

had this right, as well as high officials). Altogether, forty-five
different taxes could be levied by monasteries; taxes on hair-
cuts, on windows, on doorsteps and sills, taxes on a child or
a calf being born, taxes on a baby if it was born with double
eyelids, a sign of beauty ... The Drepung also had the right
every year during the three weeks of the great prayer festival
to send its 'iron bar lamas' – the strong-arm men of the monastery – to take over the entire administration of Lhasa municipality and impose taxes or fines at will. Nor were the lamas
as peaceful as they seemed. Huc recorded how, in Lhasa, the
monks of another great monastery, Sera, armed themselves
with spears and lances. Drepung also was not a peaceful con-
templative abode. The Chinese emperors, aware that the
monasteries, containing one-fifth of the male population, were
dangerous reservoirs of able-bodied men capable of bearing
arms, had tried to limit the number of lamas in them. Drepung,
Sera, and Gaden,[5] were limited to 7,700, 5,500 and 3,300
monks respectively. But these limits were not kept. There
were round 10,000 lamas at Drepung in 1959 and in each
monastery there were also hundreds of small boys sent at the
age of seven by their parents to become lamas and thus to
escape poverty.

In 1962 Gelder still found round about 200 such children,
ill-fed and ill-clad, in the Sera monastery. Today there are
none, not in any monastery. The supply of future lamas has
completely dried up. There were 700 monks in the big Drepung
instead of several thousand in 1962; and there were only 300
when I went to the Drepung in October 1975.

'Unwashed, insolent parasites,' was the comment of Spencer
Chapman on the lamas of Drepung. But I could not have
wished nicer monks than the dozen or so of middle-aged men,
with one or two venerable, white-haired ones, who now swept
down the glistening stone-paved path leading from the monastery to the plain, in scarlet robes, and ornate embroidered
white boots with thick soles. They greeted me affably, and
proceeded to show me everything. Their robustness was

undoubted; three were very white of skin. Tibetans of the upper classes, especially the women, shielded their faces from the sun and thus maintained a fair complexion. A mixture of grease and mutton blood, producing the 'black lacquer' which Huc had noted on the faces of women when they went out, preserved their skins. Only the serfs and slaves were burnt black by the sun.

We walked up the winding streets which led into the monastery. To right and left were houses; those of former prelates from the nobility. Each of them had a house and servants, and lived as they had always done, save for celibacy (and even celibacy had its exceptions). Up we went, climbing to the main temple, and up again by stone stairs to the great terrace upon which stood the chanting house, a magnificent structure of carmine and gold. In this courtyard, at a certain place below the steps, was a stone upon which corporal punishment was inflicted on infractors of the religion; beating with heavy wooden stakes being the usual one. 'The people did not die immediately, but 300 blows usually did finish them off; they were carried away alive, or nearly, but afterwards they died. The lamas, however, had technically not killed anyone; his death, after leaving the operative scene, was due to the will of the gods.'[6]

We walked into the vast, dim hall which occupies the lower floor of the main temple, with pillars swathed in brocades, tankas hanging, and on its stone floor the cushions where 5,000 lamas in rows knelt to pray and sing. Where I saw, at last, the Great Fifth.

For here is his bust, along with those of other great lamas and Dalai Lamas. The chanting house dates back to A.D. 1416 and an enormous fifty-foot-high Buddha is its main focus. However, so striking is the face of the Greath Fifth, that I had eyes only for it. He even eclipses the bust of Tsong Kapa, his predecessor and founder of the Yellow sect, who is also here, and whose name is an invocation, for to it are ascribed miracles and prodigies.

5

The Great Fifth has a yellow mitre, like that of a catholic bishop; a starkly aquiline nose, and vivid eyes and a mouth thin and compressed. It is the face of a fanatic, but an astute, ruthless one. Comparisons that float into the mind are those of the popes' pictures in the museums of Europe; those high prelates of the sixteenth and seventeenth centuries who were also warriors and politicians and strove to keep the power of the Church.

Of course the joyous poet, the Sixth Dalai, is missing, and the children whose demise went unexplained. The reek of butter is missing, though a faint odour comes from the amiable lamas who accompany me and open doors and pull back curtains, scaling with the agility of practice the steep, and of course, dark stairs. There is water in the silver and gold bowls set in front of the numerous statues (I have given up counting them). There is a library full of precious books, written on parchment; eagerly the lamas show me how well kept they are. Here also are painted galleries, rooms lined in gold paint, golden heads and eyes blue-rimmed, the ecstasy and the terror of the dark, the mystery of sombre trance, and I understand what Landon wrote in 1905: 'The lamas establish their domination by the terror of the supernatural.'[7] But those with me are gentle men with fine faces, neither hungry nor ill; most of them below fifty.

One lama with deft hands replaces some incense sticks in one of the chapels we pass. The odour of incense is pleasant — Tibet's incense is remarkable, and was prized above all others in the past. 'Do the deities notice that there is no more butter?' I ask as politely as I can. 'They do not seem to notice,' is the urbane reply.

Here too, the vast accumulation of treasure is slightly nauseating. It is all exacted service, corvée, squeezing grain and tribute from the terrorized people, and I agree with Dr A. L. Waddell,[8] who was chief medical officer with the Younghusband expedition and looked forward to the day when people would be freed from 'the intolerable tyranny of monks' and the devils they had invented to terrorize the people.

Here too is a chapel for Palden Lhamo, so dark as to need a torch, and the usual chaplets of skulls, which the Han Chinese found quite revolting.

'The most monstrous growth of monasticism and priestcraft the world has ever seen,' wrote O'Connor (secretary to the Younghusband expedition). He, however, thought the country well governed and the people well treated, 'as long as they confine themselves to their legitimate sphere of action (as serfs); and above all abstain from political offences (from protesting against their serfdom)'. Their rulers had 'forged innumerable weapons of servitude, invented degrading legends', and the monks were 'a host of ignorant pretentious sluggards', who officiated at births, deaths, marriages and festivals, 'and exhibited limitless—limited only by the extent of their own rapacity—ability to squeeze cash and kind in return for their religious functions.' All this was still true in 1936. 'The Lamaist monk does not spend his time in ministering to the people or educating them, nor do laymen take part in or even attend the monastery services ... Knowledge is the jealously guarded prerogative of the monasteries,' wrote Spencer Chapman then.[9] It was still true in 1950.

Up and down, down and up, to the flat top of the monastery, to see the sun go down in amethyst and scarlet and the long blue shadows of early evening creep up from the valley. The gold of the man-high conic stripes adorning the temples gives a last flash of brilliance before sudden night. It is all heart-rendingly beautiful, and heartrending. But now I am being shown the permanent exhibition in a large square room, it shows details of the conspiracy that took place, and the insurrection of 1959. Schoolchildren come here, to look at the cartoons of the Dalai Lama and the nobles, cabinet ministers, and monks, who took up arms to defy change, and lost.

I am served the best buttered tea I have ever tasted since

coming. Solicitously a lama proffers sugar, previously almost unknown in Tibet. But now sugar consumption has gone up ten times in ten years, and one finds it even in the villages. 'The Drepung lamas make the best buttered tea in Lhasa,' say my hosts. I sit back on embroidered cushion-stools and listen to Tzumen Jendze, forty-eight, but looking sixty-five. Tzumen Jendze was a 'poor lama', that is, the child of a poor family of serfs, given to the monastery to escape poverty. In the monasteries class distinctions were as rigid as outside them; a host of poor monks continued to serve, to do menial jobs, and to be beaten; but they did receive an education (religious of course), and it occasionally happened that one of them, through native intelligence and exertion, reached high rank. And then there was also the possibility of squeezing money through administering 'medical' services (for the word lama also means doctor), and of becoming holy or renowned through the good luck of 'miracles' ...

'I revolted against the lama order because I was so often flogged,' says Tzumen Jendze, who suffers from asthma. My interpreter, Dr Ma, a Muslim Tibetan, translates into Han Chinese as he speaks; she only finds difficulty when he employs religious phraseology, but that does not occur very often. Tzumen Jendze is now also chairman of the committee for the preservation and restoration of monasteries, temples and sanctuaries. There are no lay worshippers to be seen at the Drepung. According to Tzumen Jendze, 'old people' still do come, and kneel and pray, 'occasionally'.

From Tzumen Jendze, and other interviews,[10] supplemented with reading and discussions, I pried out the events leading to the flight of the Dalai Lama. Tibetans are very vague about time — in the past many people did not know their own age, since no records were kept for serfs or slaves, and also about events. Tzumen Jendze remembers vividly only the part that the Drepung took in the insurrection. 'I saw the weapons, guns and rifles come in by night. Night after night, in 1958. I was there.' They were stored 'everywhere', even behind the most

holy statues, in niches, in cellars, and in the houses of the prelates. 'And this was not only at the Drepung, but in the other
monasteries as well.' For the Drepung alone controlled seven
hundred subsidiary monasteries scattered all over Tibet and
in the Tibetan areas of adjacent provinces, and had links with
the Kantze area of Szechuan, where the Khampa rebellion
took place.

The great Drepung, birthplace of the Gelugpa Yellow Sect, had
already sent a band of fifty lamas to Chamdo in 1950 to rouse
the people against the entry of the PLA. According to Ngapo
Nawang Jigme, who was then the commander who participated in the battle against the Chinese, the monks were not
successful, because the 'battle' consisted in a series of skirmishes, which quickly subsided. Chiefly because the PLA
started caring for the wounded (it was the habit, both in warlord and Kuomintang times, and among the Tibetans, to
massacre them) and also because their impressive good behaviour towards the villagers—who fled at first, but then
returned—rapidly converted the serfs, who had never been
well treated before.[11]

After the 17-point agreement, Drepung subsided in its anti-
China activities for a while; but not for long. For now what
happened was that, although the PLA did not interfere within
Tibet itself, outside Tibet the 1,500,000 Tibetans were being
affected by the Chinese Revolution. From Mongolia in the
north to Yunnan in the south, land reform was proceeding,
more or less swiftly. And also in Tsinghai, with its majority
Tibetan population, and of course in the Chamdo territory,
still technically a part of a Chinese province until 1955. As a
result, serfs rose against their masters in these regions; monasteries though not expropriated were whittled down in their
vast powers, and their right to levy taxes; runaway slaves
were not returned to their masters. Medical teams, from the
city hospitals of China, now came on tour and started that
great—and almost unrecorded—movement for the abolition

of venereal disease, which was to take over ten years, throughout China, not excepting the minority nationalities areas, until
today it can be said that China has extirpated syphilis and
gonorrhoea.[12]

Now the pilgrimages to Lhasa, and the treasures accumulated in the monasteries thereby, came for the greater part
from these believers outside Tibet. It is therefore not surprising
that as the pilgrims dwindled, and consequently the wealth
being poured into Tibet's monasteries, the lamas grew profoundly disturbed.

The number of runaway serfs and slaves was increasing
monthly now, and the PLA fed them, clothed them, sent them,
when young, and even when middle-aged, to schools or the
Institutes of National Minorities created in several cities of
China; or employed them as road workers, handsomely paid,
or gave them simple technical courses and started to turn them
into a new class: of workers acquainted with machinery. They
did the same with the beggars, who were so numerous everywhere. The repair and maintenance teams along the new road
being built became magnets of attraction for runaway serfs
and slaves ...

And now even the sons and daughters of the nobility no
longer wanted to become lamas. Instead, they went, enthu-
siastically, to Institutes for National Minorities; they too
wanted change.

Such was the situation when, in 1954, the Dalai Lama and
the Panchen Lama both went to Peking to attend the National
People's Congress, and were received by Mao Tsetung, with
whom they had, apparently, long and friendly conversations.
Both young men professed themselves happy that the long
feuds which existed between Dalai and Panchen were now to
stop, and that harmony was restored. They and their retinues
stayed around sixteen months in China, visiting various places.
During that time, believers from Mongolia and Chinese provinces came to Peking, Anna-Louise Strong relates, and poured
gifts and gold and all they had at the feet of the Dalai Lama.

The Dalai Lama wrote, on his return, a hymn to Mao Tsetung, calling him 'The Timely Rain' (the title of Stuart Gelder's book on Tibet).[13]

The Dalai Lama and the Panchen Lama returned to Lhasa, apparently enthusiastic, and promising that reforms would happen. But not so their entourage, nor the hierarchy ...

On the way back, two of the Dalai Lama's ministers, Surkong Wongching Galeh and Tsrijong Lozong Giehsi, passing through Kantze (the Khampa district in Szechuan inhabited by Tibetans) 'instigated the local Tibetans' to revolt. Weapons were smuggled to them, from monastery to monastery. And since Kantze was a 'rich' district where commerce with the Han Chinese, and the passage of silk and tea, afforded solid cash to the lamas and nobles, an army of ten thousand Khampas was soon engaging in skirmishes, and looting and burning. The Drepung monastery had its share in the smuggling of weapons and also providing money.[14]

In 1955 the Dalai Lama proceeded on a 'shopping' expedition to India. The Chamdo region was re-attached to Tibet, since the Dalai Lama, apparently, had voiced this demand to which Mao Tsetung had acceded.[15] But this did not improve matters, quite the contrary. For Chamdo was already changing; articles of consumption were rapidly coming down in price, and this cut the profits of the lama-traders.

The Dalai Lama, it is said, complained bitterly to Nehru about changes occurring; he said there had been assaults on monasteries, and that he feared for the religion. Nehru lent a sympathetic ear to his complaints that religion was being destroyed; but advised him to return to Tibet, because Tibet was a region of China, and had never been recognized as independent. But it is probable that at the time contact with Americans was also established, through the Dalai Lama's elder brother, who had been in America and was a frequent visitor to India.

Chou En-lai's visit to India in 1955 led to a meeting with the Dalai Lama and his entourage. Although secrecy surrounded the meeting, it was apparent, from what transpired later, that some sort of compromise was achieved.

The Central Government slowed down any attempt at reforms outside Tibet. In Tsinghai (Han population 1,400,000, 400,000 Tibetans, 220,000 Huis or Muslims), a halt was called. In 1956 the Central Government was to agree that 'rash and inexperienced' young people had pushed too much change too quickly. It must be pointed out that these youths were Tibetans themselves.[16] In May 1956 the Foreign Minister, Marshal Chen Yi, went to Tibet. Chen Yi told the Tibetan cabinet that reforms would not be pressed, that 'they must come from the Tibetans themselves ... no other nationality in China can do it for them', and agreed to postponement for another six years, that is, until 1962. I saw Marshal Chen Yi on his return from Tibet, and he confirmed this. 'But the Tibetan people themselves will want reforms,' he predicted.

And it was so. 'Tibet's young people, lacking the conservatism of their elders, are jubilant at joining the age of machines and aircraft ... clamouring to go to Peking and Chengtu to study,' wrote Winnington.[17]

By 1957 the control of trade and commerce, the prerogative of nobles and lamas, was passing away from them. Cloth and manufactured goods, once exorbitant in price because of the long and costly transport on man-back and yak-back, were now coming in by lorry; whereas previously a box of matches cost a sheep, now it could be purchased at low cost. The pattern of trade was also changing; tea was now much cheaper, as were manufactured goods.

And even though the lamas did all they could to prevent the people from going to the medical teams, even lamas themselves (and photographs testify to this) went to the Han medical teams to get cured.

There was also the matter of education; although the English school established for nobles at Gyantze had failed in 1926; although a school established by the Kuomintang in the 1940s had also failed, now beggars and orphans and runaway slaves and serfs were simply being sent away to schools in China, and there was talk of opening a primary school in Lhasa.[18]

A preparatory committee for the autonomy of the region of Tibet, with the Dalai Lama and the Panchen Lama as chairman and vice-chairman respectively was set up in 1956. The Dalai Lama and the Panchen Lama now both declared themselves in favour of socialism and reform. But no reforms of any kind were ever attempted;[19] and the rebellion which was brewing among the Three Great Masters now intensified.

In 1956 I visited the Institute for National Minorities in Chengtu. There I found 2,000 students from various national minorities (there are 54 of them all told in China) and among them were several hundred Tibetans. 'What do you teach them?' I asked. 'They are mostly studying accountancy, for the agrarian reform to come,' was the reply.

Where did these young people come from? Many from the nobility, but also some were the beggars, the orphans, the slaves and serfs who had run away and had been picked up by the PLA.

'You cannot stay for ever on a yak's back,' one of these students (of noble family) said to Winnington.[20]

Meanwhile, plotting intensified, and now with the connivance (or laissez-faire) of India. American agents in Kalimpong made contact with disgruntled Tibetan nobles and lamas. Weapons came in, smuggled by all available means. Between 1957 and 1958, there was parachuting of guns, and also of trained guerrillas, into Tibet.[21] By all the passes which cross into Tibet, Tibetans from over the border came in; many had been induced to become 'agents', but one doubts whether they were efficient. In 1958, the Americans, with the advice of Lowell Thomas, tried to instigate the Dalai Lama to appeal openly for American intervention. 'I did not think before March 1959 that we had *direct* contact with the Americans,' the Dalai Lama was to say in an interview in Dharamsala, India, in August 1975. But his elder brother was certainly a contact.

In 1955, in Lithang valley, the Chinese had begun to levy taxes on the smugglers and traders coming into Tibet from India. Lithang had a monastery which lived on 'trade' of this kind. It housed 5,000 monks and had 113 satellite monasteries. The lamas attacked the Han garrison in Lithang. Khampas from Kantze then sent a delegation to Lhasa, which was housed in the Drepung monastery. In 1958, the Drepung monastery sent around 3,000 armed men to Loka, to organize a 'Support Religion' army.

The lamas now embarked in a campaign against the Hans with strong religious appeal. 'All of us were told that, if we killed a Han, we would become living Buddhas and have chapels to our name,' said Tzumen Jendze. 'They told us that lorries and trucks were fed on the blood of children taken away by the Hans,' said Tandzemolo, an ex-lama now a mechanic.[22]

In early 1959, Drepung, as well as the other two large monasteries of the Lhasa valley, Sera and Gaden, helped to call the 'peoples' conference' in the Norbulingka palace which was to promote the armed rebellion of March 1959.

The Indian government was quite aware of what was going on; the appearance, in the *Statesman* of March 2, 1959, of a prediction of the coming putsch, even stated that the Dalai Lama would be taken out of Lhasa on March 17 — which turned out to be correct.

At the end of February 1959, four out of the six ministers in the cabinet of the Dalai Lama had joined the conspiracy. A rapid escalation began in Lhasa itself.

On March 1, the Dalai Lama had been invited by the Chinese garrison commander, General Tan Kuan-san, to a theatrical entertainment at his headquarters, on March 10. He was also invited to attend the National People's Congress, to be held in Peking in April, since he was the representative of Tibet to the Congress. At the time the Dalai Lama was at his summer palace at the Norbulingka, where the confederates had their headquarters. On March 10, monks from the three

.monasteries came out as armed men, and joined the small Tibetan army. They set up mortars and machine guns facing the headquarters of the PLA, and also road blocks, surrounding the Chinese garrison. There were now 10,000 insurgents. Meanwhile other lamas spread among the people, until a crowd of round 30,000 surrounded the Norbulingka, shouting: 'The Hans must go.'

Then came the episode of letters exchanged between the Dalai Lama and General Tan Kuan-san.

The original letters from the Dalai Lama are in the State archives, with photocopies exhibited in the museums in Lhasa. The first dated March 11 says: 'I intended to ... see the theatrical performance yesterday, but I was unable to do so, because of obstruction by people, lamas and laymen, who were instigated by a few evil elements and who did not know the facts ... Reactionary, evil elements are carrying out activities endangering me under the pretext of ensuring my safety. I am taking measures to calm things down ... ' The letter was in reply to a brief note from General Tan, who, on March 10, because of the disturbances wrote to the Dalai Lama, 'since the intrigues and provocations of the reactionaries have caused you great difficulties, it may be advisable that for the time being you do not come.' The subsequent explanation by the Dalai Lama, that the people feared he would be abducted by the Chinese, and hence surrounded the Norbulingka to defend him, appears an afterthought.

On the 11th, General Tan wrote to the Dalai Lama that the highway north of the Norbulingka had been blocked by the rebels. On March 12 the Dalai replied that 'the unlawful activities of the reactionary clique cause me endless worry and sorrow' and that some Tibetan army men had 'fired shots' along the highway. On March 15 General Tan, who was by now aware that four of the six ministers of the cabinet were siding with the rebels, expressed concern about the Dalai Lama's safety and invited him to 'extricate yourself from your present dangerous position' and to come to stay for a short time in the military area command. This message was passed by Ngapo Nawang Jigme.

On March 10, the very day of the theatrical performance, the 'people's conference' under the auspices of the grand secretary of the cabinet had proclaimed Tibet's independence.[23] A captured document which later fell in the hands of the PLA[24] revealed that the Dalai Lama became genuinely angry at this; hence for a long time the Chinese believed that he had been forced to flee against his will, abducted by his own entourage. And indeed the tenor of his letters, including the last one, dated March 16, the day before he fled, seems to indicate this. In his last letter of March 16 the Dalai Lama states he made a speech to 'more than seventy' government officials, asking them to calm down, and promising 'in a few days' to come to the Chinese military area command.

By March 17 it was all over. The Dalai Lama writes that the boom of heavy mortar shells outside the *north* gate of the Norbulingka, falling into a pond, convinced him that his life was in danger. The Chinese have denied that they fired any mortar shells, or any ammunition, until March 20; and since it was the insurgents who were holding a blockade of the road north of the Norbulingka it is possible that the mortars (and they had mortars) were theirs. But the terrified young man now feared for his life; and it was decided (or perhaps it was decided for him) that he should flee.

The Dalai Lama has described in moving terms how he rose that night, and with his family made his way across the Kyi river (tributary of the Yalutsangpo, and on which Lhasa is situated) in a coracle. On the other side horses were waiting for him; to carry him, his family, his retinue, to India. In this flight he was joined by four out of six of his ministers; and later by many thousands of nobles and upper prelates, including 500 from the Drepung. Altogether round 13,000 people left within the week.

On April 2 the Dalai Lama reached the frontier with India; the exact spot, and time of arrival, was broadcast by Radio

Peking. Throughout his fifteen-day journey, the Chinese knew exactly where he was, and how he proceeded. No attempt was made to pursue him.

'Why did you let the Dalai Lama go?' I asked, out of curiosity, Prime Minister Chou En-lai in November 1959.

He replied that the situation was complex; at the time they felt the Dalai Lama 'might have been forced to run away by his entourage'. They were right, since his letters to General Tan Kuan-san show plainly that he was not in agreement with the insurgents, who had occupied his palace and made it their headquarters. 'And besides,' said Prime Minister Chou En-lai to me, 'any action might have endangered the Dalai Lama's life. We did not wish to hinder him or to put his life in danger.'

Forty-eight hours after his departure, fighting took place in Lhasa. The rebel troops, strengthened with fighting monks, opened fire with machine-guns, mortars and rifles; attacking the Chinese military area command from the Potala, the Norbulingka, from the Jokka Kang, where they also ensconced machine-gun nests, and from the Sera monastery on Iron Hill, a prominence facing the Potala and commanding a view of the whole city of Lhasa.

The attack began round 4 a.m. on March 20. The Chinese garrison, which had confined the soldiers to barracks and dug shelters against sniper fire, did not reply until 10 a.m. At 10 a.m., a radio directive from Peking, which had ascertained that the Dalai Lama was not exposed to any danger, gave the order to counter-attack. This began with the storming by a PLA company of Iron Hill; the commanding point was taken in three hours. From Iron Hill the PLA moved on to the Norbulingka and by seven in the evening had cleared it of insurgents. Then came the clean-up of Lhasa. This took one day, the 21st; the fiercest fighting was at the temple of Ramogia. By nightfall only the Potala and the Jokka Kang were held by the conspirators. Instead of storming these, the PLA now went over to a political campaign. Ngapo Nawang Jigme, and Sampo

Tsewang-rentzen, the two out of the six ministers who did not join the conspiracy, used loudspeakers to call for surrender; and by nine the next morning the last rebels had surrendered. During the next two weeks, a clean-up for thirty miles round Lhasa was performed.

From the Drepung, according to Tzumen Jendze, 500 top prelates all joined the conspirators; and with them 4,000-odd lama-soldiers. 'But quite a few, like myself, did not join the rebels.'

On March 28, the Dalai Lama's cabinet was dissolved, and authority in Tibet vested in the preparatory committee inaugurated in 1956. The Dalai Lama remained titular head of Tibet, and chairman of the preparatory committee. On April 18, the Dalai Lama was even re-elected vice-chairman of the standing committee of the National People's Congress in Peking. It took some years for the Central Government to abrogate these titles.

Now the monasteries were entered. 'The PLA came to Drepung and told all the lamas that if they wanted to leave, they could. All the children and many young lamas left. Those who had no families were collected in orphanages and sent to school.' The hidden weapons were found. And now expropriation began. All the land belonging to the nobles who had taken part in the rebellion, and the land of the great monasteries, were confiscated without compensation and distributed to their serfs.

In the Loka area, where Drepung had sent men and support, the rebellion was dispersed within a fortnight. Around 10,000 Khampas did continue fighting and looting, until they filtered through the border. Including lamas, nobles, their retinues, and the Khampas, a maximum figure of 30,000 probably crossed into India and Nepal and Kashmir; the Chinese made no move to restrain them (I think they felt it good riddance). Outside Tibet the Khampas would be supported with weapons and money to launch guerrilla raids—ineffectual—on unfortunate merchants and tradesmen, since there were no Chinese

convoys on the roads to India. Mr George N. Patterson, a confirmed anti-China man, took a BBC crew, it appears, to film
such a 'raid' ... from India. The authenticity of such pictures is
questionable. It brought, however, Mr Patterson's expulsion
both from India and from Nepal.

But all this ceased abruptly when American policy towards
China changed in 1972. Just as the Kuomintang remnants in
Laos had turned into bandits and opium smugglers maintained
by the CIA, so the Khampas turned into a major nuisance; and
in 1974 the Nepalese government sent troops to dislodge them
from border areas in Nepal where they were terrorizing
villages.

In 1975, leaving the Drepung monastery, with the monks
waving goodbye in the dusk, I saw it as it had become, a
museum piece. Probably it is so with the other 2,711 monasteries, emasculated of power and the ability to terrorize the
people. The 300 lamas left in Drepung still own 1,000 sheep,
100 milch cows, some yaks, and about 50 acres of land upon
which they plant fruit trees which they sell; they made 6,000
yuan in 1974 out of selling fruit. They also receive small pensions from the government. But the dread edifice of the theocracy is truly gone. The smiling, gentle monks I met, in their
wine-coloured gowns, know it well. I did not ask them
whether they regretted the past. It would have been rude.
Perhaps their faith helps them to endure with fortitude their
diminished state; the fortitude they preached so abundantly,
for so many centuries, to the thousands of serfs and slaves who
made their existence, and its comforts, so outrageously secure.

4

The Serfs

The triumph of the Chinese Revolution was due in great part to the fact that Mao Tsetung forged a revolutionary army, the PLA, into a political and educational force, a 'work and construction' force; as well as the military arm of the Communist Party. The army was, as Mao said after the Long March, a 'seeding machine', sowing consciousness, revolt, among the oppressed and the exploited. It was also 'a great school for cadres'. The word cadre means administrator, and includes doctors, mechanics, engineers, intellectuals of all sorts, all those whose function involves stimulating, educating, leading. The drastic distinction which the West makes, between military and civilian, does not exist in a China where the Revolution was twenty-two years of armed struggle, and every cadre, in 1949, was also a PLA man, or had done some work with the army — even writers, musicians and actors.

In Tibet, as in other areas inhabited by the national minorities, the strategy of transformation involved, first of all, arousing the serfs and slaves, training, as swiftly as possible, thousands of 'cadres' among them. This was Mao Tsetung's line, and 'it has been followed in Tibet'.[1] Had the PLA come in as an alien ruler, imposing change however beneficial but estranged from the local people, it would have failed. But there was patience, and consummate psychology, in the army's behaviour. In every sector I studied, I could see the evidence of active, even enthusiastic cooperation elicited from the Tibetans themselves. 'Political indoctrination?' To involve people in their own self-change; to persuade them of their human dignity, is the

6

key factor in this indoctrination. 'We saw there was another
way of living. Another existence than the one we had.' 'We
understood it was not the will of the Gods, but the cruelty of
men like ourselves, which kept us slaves.'

I interview Tsomo, a beautiful woman of thirty-four, and a
Memba, from a border region in Tibet.[2] 'My family were serfs,
so poor I was farmed out to work for another family. When I
was seventeen, the lamas told us to run away into the mountains because the Hans were coming and would kill, rape, eat
the children. We ran and hid in the cliffs. And we saw Chingdrolmami arrive.'

Chingdrolmami is the Tibetan name for the PLA.

'The soldiers camped near our village. We expected them to
take away everything, to burn our fields and houses; but after
a day or two, we saw they did not touch our fields. So I came
down a little lower, to watch them.

'They were working; I know now they were making a
road, but away from our fields. I could not understand. My
mother said: "Don't go, don't go," but I came down again the
next day, and I saw among them women in uniform. One of
them perceived me, hiding behind a rock, and called to me in
my own language to come down, not to be afraid. She was a
woman interpreter.'

Tsomo came down, and was given food, water, and told not
to be frightened. 'The Hans told me they had come to build
a road. I saw then that they had fed and milked the cows,
and taken nothing. They gave me milk and butter to take
back, and food. I returned and told my mother, but she
would not believe me. "This is a trick; when we come
down they will kill us." But two young boys believed
me, and came down with me the next day. And they also
believed the Hans, and the three of us went back to the
mountain to tell the others; and in a week all our village came
down.'

After that there was no stopping Tsomo. 'Chingdrolmami
treated us well; did not beat or shout; helped us with the

reaping and threshing; never looked at the women. Never had anyone been like this to us before. My heart began to glow with a great fire. I wanted to be like them. I told them: "What can I do to help?" An officer said to me: "Would you like to learn something? To read and to write?" I had never dreamt this could happen.

'My mother stopped saying: "This is a trick." And Ching-drolmami told me they would send me to school in the inland. My mother at first did not want me to go; but later she said yes, and I went.'

Thus, out of serfdom, Tsomo became a student at the Institute of National Minorities in Peking. Today she is vice-chairman of the woman's federation in Tibet, and a 'leader' cadre. She returned to lead the land reform in her district; going from village to village, rousing the serfs. 'I organized a mutual aid team, and I also organized the women serfs. We Tibetan women do most of the heavy labour except plough-ing; so they listened to me.'

Then in 1964 she was a delegate at the all-China conference of national minorities; 'I could not believe this was true; the tears flowed from my eyes. I felt one life was not enough to do something to repay all that happiness.' She saw Chairman Mao, and right in the hall burst into an impromptu song – for Tsomo is also a gifted singer. Since then she has visited five provinces and many Tibetan counties 'inland', singing her song and stirring up the people.

I interview Kawa, aged forty-four, previously a slave, now a worker in the repair and maintenance factory for motorized vehicles of Lhasa.

'My grandfather and my father were slaves; my father wore iron on his legs for debts. We had only rags. I did not know what a blanket was. I cut wood for the master when I was eight years old, and between eight and twenty-five, I was sold four times to four different lords. I ate with the dogs and slept with them for warmth.'

Kawa looks his life; he appears to be sixty; his frame is

stunted, his bones knobbly, his face hewn with wrinkles. 'One spring, when I was twenty-five, I saw Chingdrolmami arrive. I saw the first bulldozer! I had never seen one before, and I thought: "This is a new monster, this is a new god." So I went down on my knees and worshipped it, hoping it would spare my life.'

But as the days went by, Kawa saw the road being built; and the first lorries, carrying supplies and men. 'I saw the men climb on the backs of these monsters, which were their servants.' He waited through summer and autumn, and one cold night, watching from afar, he had had enough of hunger, of cold, of being beaten. 'I had never seen the face of my master; no slave would dare to lift his eyes upon the master's face. If he did he was flogged, or if the master were cruel, he would have an eye torn out.'

And then a lorry stopped, not too far from where Kawa crouched, watching. 'The driver was doing something to the engine; I crept up, and climbed into it, and hid among bags. He did not see me. All night it rolled, and at dawn stopped; it was a Han soldier camp. They found me. I said: "Please do not return me to my master." They said: "You must learn something else than always being afraid."'

Kawa was fed, clothed; for weeks he wandered round the soldiers' camp, boiling water, carrying wood, doing odd jobs. 'They tried to teach me but it was very difficult. I could not learn; too many beatings.' But in 1962 he was assigned to the factory, where he works on a simple machine. 'In 1964 I became a delegate for my people at the National People's Congress and I went to Peking. I shook hands with Chairman Mao. Just imagine!' And Kawa burst into tears.

Kawa is still illiterate, despite years of trying; but he is a forceful, moving speaker. I asked him: 'Would you like the Dalai Lama to return?'

Kawa stared at me as if I were mad. 'In 1965 I became a Party member; I married in 1969 and I have three children. I have a flat, good food three times a day, I saw Chairman Mao three times. Why should I want Hell back? Every day now is Paradise to me.'

Another witness, Pasang, a woman, vice-chairman of the revolutionary committee for the whole of Tibet, leader of a delegation to Japan in 1975. 'I was a slave from Kongka, born in a family of slaves for five generations. I became a servant in the master's house when I was nine years old. I was ill-treated, beaten, often I ate the garbage, I was so hungry. Then I heard about Chingdrolmami; I was then thirteen. "If you go to them, they will not send you back to the master." ' Pasang ran away, wandered for five days and nights, hiding in the hills, going down to the valley fields to eat some raw peas and barley by night. 'At last I found Chingdrolmami.' She also went to the Institute for National Minorities; learnt both Tibetan and Han; came back three years later and plunged into land reform. She became mayor of her district, Langhsien, organized 1,500 men as road-builders—she was their foreman—is now one of the four top Tibetan leaders of the revolutionary committee for the whole of Tibet. (Four others are Han.)

Also Jedi, handsome, in his early thirties, secretary of the Party in Tibet. 'I come from the Shantang plateau, the high pastures of the north, 4 to 5 kilometres above sea-level. We have beautiful horses there. I was a slave herdsman, as my father was, for the monastery. Had it not been for the Party and Chairman Mao, what would I be?' Jedi is, of course, a fervent communist.

Ishichiangtsai, thirty-eight, saw his father killed in front of him by the lord serf-owner. 'When I was eighteen the PLA came, and I went to school and learnt to read.' He is now a doctor in a commune near Tsushui, 100 kilometres from Lhasa. He, too, shows past suffering in his face.

And Ridjin Wangyal, of Nyambad commune, very near the 'MacMahon line' in south-east Tibet, reputedly the most advanced agricultural unit in the region. 'I was only a talking animal.' His master sent him to work on the road the PLA was building—this apparently was what some serf-owners did—

and then collected all the money that he earned.[3] 'Serfs were born with a whip over their heads ... but during the six months I worked on the road, I was treated like a human being.' A PLA Han soldier working by his side gave him water to drink out of his own cup. 'I could not believe it!!' Nor could he believe it when he received money, wages. He had never seen money before. Although he kept it only a short while since it was confiscated by his owner. When 1959 came, and the Dalai Lama had gone, 'we serfs rose like fire against our owners'.

It is not true that there were never any serf revolts before the Revolution came to Tibet. There had been uprisings, in 1908, 1918, 1931, and in the 1940s; tax-gatherers were sometimes killed by angry serfs. But these revolts were swiftly and brutally crushed; this was easy, due to the scanty population, the armed retainers of the serf-owners, including monasteries, and the vast distances between the villages.

The PLA roadbuilders did not stop when they reached Lhasa in 1954. They pushed westwards, southwards, right to the Himalayas and across the grasslands; building 16,000 kilo-metres between 1954 and 1974, with Lhasa as the hub of a new transport and communication system linking 72 out of 73 of Tibet's counties (bar the county of Nieramu, near Nepal).[4] Everywhere the road went, there sprang up activists, potential cadres, revolutionaries. The seeding machine seeded; and in turn each Tibetan thus set afire set others afire ... and thus land reform was not done by the Hans, but by the Tibetan serfs themselves, led by the Tibetans returned from the Institutes of National Minorities, several hundreds of them.

Winnington reckoned in 1955 that out of the approximately one million Tibetans in Tibet, 600,000 were agricultural serfs, 200,000 pastoral serfs, while there were 150,000 monks,[5] and 50,000 'nobility, merchants, artisans, and beggars [sic!]'. Of these 50,000, only 200 families were rich nobles and serf-owners, which means, at the most, stretching each family to include 50 people, a total of 10,000. Beggars were rife in every city, and if we say there were 20,000 beggars (and there were surely more, from all accounts) that leaves us with 20,000 artisans and traders, the latter a fluid quantity, since the nobles and lamas were merchant-traders. In 1975 I was told that 'only 626 people in all held 93 per cent of the land and the wealth, and 70 per cent of the cattle, in Tibet'. These 626 comprised 333 heads of the monasteries, and religious authorities, and 287 lay authorities which included the nobles in the Tibetan army (officers) and 6 cabinet ministers.

Again instead of 200,000 pastoral serfs, there were, in 1974, 340,000 'people engaged in livestock occupations and 800,000 people engaged in agricultural occupations'. Since the population has increased from less than a million in 1949 to 1,345,000 Tsang, and 100,000 'other ethnic groups',[6] the population increase accounts for some of these figures; but also a new definition of 'livestock occupation'. Serfs, agricultural or pastoral, often owned one cow, a couple of sheep, occasionally a yak (though most of the yaks, being transport and ploughing animals, were owned either by merchants or serf-owners). Even in the agricultural communes of today there is always a strong livestock unit; for there are today 10 to 12 times more sheep, cows, yaks, than there are people. The distinction between pastoral and agricultural serfs is therefore confusing.

Winnington gives some hair-raising figures[7] of what it meant, in economic terms, to be a serf. Every serf, even if he owned at least one cow, or a couple of sheep, as his own 'property', had to rent land from the lords, or the monasteries, to labour on; there was actually no 'free' land, since even if a serf ran away to settle on unclaimed land and cultivate it, it was ultimately annexed by the serf-owners. Approximately only 25 per cent of the value of all he produced by his labour was retained by him. The rest went into tribute, rent, *corvée*, ula at his master's pleasure. Even when freed from any debt, he retained, at most, one-third of the total value of his labour. Entire villages were bought or sold; a custom which need not astonish us, since it was practised in Europe until fairly recently, and in Russia till the twentieth century.

'Land reform from 1959, the year when democratic reforms could begin, has been throughout an arduous, and complex class struggle,' said Tien Pao, a Tibetan, vice-commander of the PLA in Tibet, vice-chairman of the revolutionary committee for the Autonomous Region of Tibet.

When land reform took place, beginning in the autumn of 1959, I am certain that there were 'excesses'. These have been magnified by the Dalai Lama; horrendous reports of murders etc., involving the monasteries and the 200 families (and remember that Drepung monastery owned 40,000 serfs) have all been publicized as 'atrocities' committed by the Hans. The facts are that expropriation of the monasteries took place; expropriation of the serf-owners took place; those who had been involved in the 1959 conspiracy were expropriated without compensation; those who had not with compensation. In such an enormous revolt, an earthquake of change, it would be incredible if there had not been some 'excesses'. Revenge is a human trait; and it is strange that what the Tibetan people endured at the hands of their rulers has never been mentioned as 'atrocity'.

In one way, land reform in Tibet was easier than in China; for here class distinctions between lord and serf, serf-owner and those who toiled for him, were rigidly marked; whereas in a Chinese clan village—as most Chinese villages are—the landlord often bears the same name as the tenant he exploits. In Tibet there are no family names; there seldom are in a slave society; where serfs are subject even in their marital unions to the lord's will, the notion of family is disintegrated by the fact that any member of it can be sold at any time by the owner. But in another way, reforms of any kind were exceedingly complex because of the depth and emotional strength of religious superstition, and conservatism, in the minds of the serfs.

For every gesture, action, was also ritual; demons lurked behind each tree, and each stone; to be placated always. The earth was divine ground, and deep ploughing forbidden; canals were not dug because 'divine streams' could not be touched. It was an intangible world of taboos, stronger than any material obstacle, which also had to be changed.

Photographs of the serfs holding mass meetings which were taken at the time are usually dismissed as 'propaganda', and the few reports do not convey the intensity of what took place, the emotions aroused, the outpourings of that vast accumulation of inhumanity which was the old Tibetan rule. There were certainly also pitched battles, armed assaults; for the nobles and the monasteries fought back, and they were armed and numerous.

There was also trouble in the Institutes of National Minorities themselves; troubles due to the fact that the sons and daughters of nobles admitted—and there were many—were now faced with a dilemma, for land reform affected their own families. One of the two ministers who became a chief rebel leader, Surkong Wongching Galeh instigated rebellion among these youths when he returned from Peking in 1955; he and Tsrijong Lozong Giehsi were also the ones responsible for stirring up the Kantze district in Szechuan. This ill-documented revolt among the young was also 'class struggle', and the serfs, slaves, beggars who attended the Institutes 'thus gained a great political lesson in class struggle'. Until 1966, and the Cultural Revolution, this division among the young trained to carry out reforms would persist; along lines similar to the 'two-line struggle' in China against Liu Shao-chi.[8] It involved the whole course of development, in all sectors, and it was the Cultural Revolution which solved this problem in Tibet, as it solved it in China.

The agriculture of Tibet was a 'subsistence agriculture', with low production, primitive instruments (light wooden ploughs, not iron-tipped, for iron was not only expensive but 'malefic'). There was no notion of wages or even of yields as we measure them. No agricultural improvement at first seemed possible, even after land reform had redistributed land among the serfs, and debts had been automatically cancelled. Although land was plentiful, it is estimated that only 5 per cent of cultivable land was cultivated in 1959. Every serf household had to supply at least one person full time for ula or *corvée*, to monastery or serf-owners. When the serfs were liberated, the creation of mutual-aid teams was urgent. Even before land reform in the period 1956 to 1959, loans, interest free, were being distributed in the ten counties ruled by the Panchen Lama[9] to relieve distress; chiefly in the form of good, clean seed, but also in money, interest free.

No agricultural teaching class could be held since the serfs could not read; and the population density was so low that it would have been necessary to collect them over a wide area in lorries to do so. They were not used to discussing matters which to them were almost religious ritual; planting, harvesting, reaping; all done with religious formulas muttered at the time (invocations to the gods and to Tsong Kapa) to help gather a good crop.

The result was that in the sector of agriculture Tibet has been a deficit area till 1974; costing the Central Government a good deal of money – 'State granted funds have made up the greater part of the region's revenue,' said the forthright Tien Pao in 1975.[10] The amount spent on water conservancy projects, disease prevention, measures for livestock, relief in distressed areas, public health, culture, and education, is not known, but it must be considerable. And although there were cattle, the switch-over to collective livestock breeding with 30 per cent of the cattle, sheep, horses, and yaks still private property was also difficult.

Although over the years butter was no longer to be burnt before the gods in the temples, the amount of waste, in butter, leather and wool was still considerable. There were also no chemical fertilizers; human manure was used; the amount of animal droppings – with the ten million or more livestock – was large, but used for fuel chiefly and much of it wasted because scarcity of population did not allow for manual collecting, since livestock roam about freely, and there never were enclosed pastures. Whereas in the well-peopled provinces of China, improvement of soil, afforestation, water-conservancy projects could be done with the abundant manpower, without machinery, here, with less than one person per square kilometre, this was quite impossible.

But with all these problems, there was also the will to change. New experimental stations for agriculture were set up in Shigatze and Lhasa in 1953, and also in reclaimed unwanted land; these have now become State farms, of which there are twelve in Tibet, tilled by the PLA in its road building – since the PLA did not live off Tibetan agriculture and since the country, already deficient in food, was quite incapable of supporting even another 100,000 men (supporting, as it did, an army of 140,000 idle lamas and nobles). 'Our Han brothers never took anything from the people; on the contrary, they gave food away from their own fields.' This is where the PLA, as a 'work and production force' proved a powerful engine of change. For it is in the State farms they inaugurated, in the research stations which were sited there, that a dozen agronomists from the Chinese cities first started experiments on seeds (they were sixty, with forty-five Tibetan trainees, by 1956). And they found that, contrary to what was imbedded assumption, the soil of Tibet was excellent, the crops as good, if not better than those in China, provided fertilizer was added; that most of the valleys had a southerly aspect and that the blazing sun 'makes vegetables grow two or three times the size that we get in the lowlands'. Hence the growing of succulent tomatoes, which I saw, at 13,000 feet. Hence the enormous cabbages, turnips, carrots.

Eighty-four different types of crops, and 440 varieties of seed were now tested, tried, and adapted to the altitude, between 1953 and 1959. A Shansi province type of wheat, strong in the stalk,[11] was evolved, which one now finds in the Lhasa valley. 'But it took a little time to persuade our Tibetan brothers to plant wheat. They were not accustomed to anything but buckwheat and barley.' And obviously, nothing could be done with the small, scattered individual farms, even if production was raised (by round 8 per cent or so) when mutual teams came into existence in some areas in 1960. It was only when the communes started to come into being, in 1965, that the plan for boosting agricultural production could really take shape.

I visited the communes in the Lhasa valley; large in size, weak in people; a startling contrast to the communes in Szechuan.

It was not until 1967, during the Cultural Revolution that communes became widespread in Tibet. Today, save for certain border areas, all the rural countryside has communes.

During the period 1959–67, after land reform gave land to the serfs, individual farming led, as in China, to polarization. Individual families differed in skill and strength; drought, illness and funerals (which are very costly) imposed their own inequalities; the serfs were unaccustomed to individual farming, unaccustomed to planning or saving; religious fear and superstition, a nefarious influence and a new landlordism – as in China between 1952 and 1956 – cropped up.

The 'three abolitions' movement, anti-insurrection, anti-ula, anti-serfdom, led by the returned students from the Institutes of National Minorities had, however, produced a crop of new recruits to Revolution from the newly liberated serfs and herdsmen. One asset was the Tibetan women. The woman in Tibet is *the* heavy labourer in rural areas; she does everything except ploughing. It is she who milks, churns the milk into butter, threshes and reaps, drives in the cattle, grinds and parches the barley, collects yak-dung (a very expensive item of fuel). Besides ploughing, grooming horses, hunting, and herding sheep, men do the stitching and are craftsmen or hunt. Women workers also carry stones for house building, men do the woodwork. No wonder all photographs of land reform accusing serf-owners and making flaming speeches show women serfs in vast numbers.

The commune in Tibet is at two levels only: the production

team, or village, and the commune, with occasionally an inter-
calary *chu* or district in between, instead of the brigade found
in China. Unlike China, agricultural communes in the Lhasa
valley have abundant grazing land, since there are too few
people to cultivate the available land. In the communes of
today each family has a private plot, sheep, a cow or two, a
yak or a horse—sometimes two—hens, and also sometimes
pigs.

The average commune in Lhasa valley will have round a
thousand people for a vast amount of land. Thus in Tetzin
county, which I visited, there are 27,000 'mouths'—men,
women and children—in 35 communes. In Tsushui county 17
communes gather only 21,000 people of whom 18,000 are
Tibetans, 3,000 are Hans or 'other'.[12] Nearly half the Tibetans
are under 16, for Tsushui health programme is a model, with
100 per cent of the children covered by preventive innocula-
tions and antenatal and maternity care in each commune
here.

Lhasa's countryside is really beautiful; flanking valleys frame
the light flooding from the splendid sky; there is the immediacy
of piercing vision rendered more so by the gladdening sight,
along the road, of brightly clad women and white-shirted
men working in groups, digging canals under a small plan-
tation of red flags whipping in the wind. There were also
banners inscribed in Han and Tibetan: 'FOLLOW THE EXAMPLE
OF TACHAI[13]—BUILD A NEW TIBET'.

By luck my visit to Lhasa was a month after the departure
of Mr Hua Kuo-feng, recently Prime Minister, leading the
delegation from the Central Government come to congratulate
the region on the tenth anniversary of its autonomy (proclaimed in September 1965). Mr Hua Kuo-feng had been in
charge of implementing the vigorous agricultural programme
for accelerated mechanization of agriculture in China. And in
Tibet too, everywhere, I heard 'Mechanization of agriculture
within five years (by 1980) in Tibet!'

And so, in the lovely morning, and after the heat of the day, there were the production teams, barley harvest done, making new fields, and digging small canals, for water.

But mechanization within five years? I walked the footpaths crossing fields of barley, towards a pretty, sheer-white village, whitewashed and sparkling, jet-black yaks sunning against the white walls. In a field three men were ploughing with yaks. I noticed that the ploughs were now iron-tipped, and instead of pushing them (as was done before when the yaks pushed the plough forward with their lowered heads, surely a most in-efficient way of making a furrow not more than four inches deep) the yaks were now *pulling* the plough. This was already innovation. The men greeted me jovially, obligingly paused for photographs; not so obligingly the yaks. They have a ten-dency to glare, and then to charge at strange people. And apparently they are unable to plough more than half a day. But the female produces, every day, 2 lbs of concentrated thick buttery milk.

Beyond us more fields stretched shimmering with delicate green, the winter wheat. The men explained they would sow wheat on the fields they were ploughing. The barley, staple food, had already been reaped; and I passed women using loose-headed flails, throwing grain in the air, near a great barn of honey-coloured barley stalks. They sang as they worked. In the distance, a single tractor was busy, opening up more ploughed land; in a mud-walled enclosure were young trees; for reafforestation of this bare valley is also in the programme and trees must be kept safe from the many animals that would otherwise eat the saplings.

I will not attempt to give measures of yield of barley or wheat, for what with the translation from Tibetan to Chinese of weights and land measures by my very able interpreter, the Muslim Tibetan doctor Mao Feng-pi, and what with the fact that the *k'e* measure of weight of grain was also the amount of land needed to produce a k'e, just as the word ula means labour for the lord and the whimsical pittance re-ceived for it, I got very confused, while my Tibetan friends grinned with unfeigned pleasure at having made things so clear.

After a twenty-minute walk through the fields, we had reached the village, and were sitting in the house of Tzemu, a wizened little man of forty-two. His house was clean; one large room. By it, the stable or cow-byre; hens cackling in the small courtyard, whitewashed walls. Inside a large low bed for the family covered with an old, faded rug, a table, one of the walls pasted with newspaper, the *Lhasa Daily*. His second wife, twenty-eight, looked forty and was nursing her last, two-year-old child, a hefty boy. Long suckling till three to four years of age, is the practice here. Tzemu had eight children by his first wife, who died. 'All of us want many children, many children,' said Tzemu proudly. I heard this many times in Tibet, where the Tibetans have become extremely conscious of their diminutive population, and where demographic expansion is encouraged, as it is in all the minorities. For whereas the Han majority (92 per cent of the 800 million) practise birth control very strictly now (no more than two children per family) there is no birth control at all, by Central Government policy, among the minorities and certainly not in Tibet. 'We want many more Tibetans, a healthy population.'[14]

Tzemu rambled, jumping from one topic to the other. All my interviews were to be like that, delightfully discursive, for here was no staleness, no prepared speech, no prepared notes, this was the first time in their lives that almost all those I saw had ever been interviewed. Tzemu wanted to speak about mechanization. 'In five years, our production team will also have a tractor.' It appeared the tractor I had perceived did not belong to his village, but to another commune, but here eyesight is so acute, distances deceiving. The tractor was actually two miles away.

'So you are no longer afraid of machines?' Tzemu laughed, talked to his wife, who kept on protruding her tongue gently at me, a sign of high courtesy in Tibet. 'We were afraid at first, but not now.' He explained that his eldest son was training to be a tractor driver. 'All the young Tibetans love machinery, they all want to drive tractors or cars or lorries, or to become workers,' said my hosts to me later.

'How are you going to buy them?' Tzemu's team (called the third production team of Sanmu commune) is saving money for mechanization. The commune has already accumulated 25,000 yuan for the purpose. This seems incredible because it only has 197 families and less than 1,000 mouths; Tzemu's team only has 185 people, of whom 94 are 'labour force', 91 under 14, or too old to work.

Tzemu and his wife were serfs under different lords. He was in debt, which increased every year as the interest was so high (to be paid in grain, double the amount at year's end from what he borrowed). After land reform he received land; then came the communes, and then the workpoint. 'This came with the Cultural Revolution,' said Tzemu, who was a bit vague on dates. Now the workpoint average, per day, was 1·25 to 1·50 yuan, higher than in my province of Szechuan, where the workpoint average is 70 to 80 cents. Tzemu said that the commune had grown rich because 'the government buys with good money' and bought wool and hides and meat. The commune sold eggs and vegetables, the tax was low, many things were free, such as medical care, schools, and seeds (wheat).[15] 'All this did not exist before.' So the small team had accumulated in its savings fund about 4,500 yuan, and of the 36 families in this team, 35 had some savings, from 10 to 100 yuan, one had none. 'Why?' 'Because of a funeral,' said Tzemu.

Funerals are still expensive. In Lhasa valley, the custom is 'heavenly burial'. The dead are taken to a high mountain, there professional undertakers cut up the body, and give the flesh to eat morsel by morsel to the birds of the air; particularly a kind of bearded vulture which abounds. In the past a family used to get into ruinous debt when there was a funeral. Illness was also very expensive; the lamas exacted, to 'exorcise the demons of disease', grain and butter, and sometimes sheep.

Several communes later, I found that on the average the

1 View of Lhasa valley from the roof of the Potala

2 Ploughing with yaks in the Lhasa valley

3 Women digging an irrigation canal

4 The author visiting a commune's new irrigation canal

5 Statue of King Songtsang Kampo at the Jokka Kang

6 Statues lining the corridors in the Jokka Kang

7 The Dalai Lama's bed at the Potala

8 Great statue of Buddha in the Jokka Kang

9 Golden roofs of the Jokka Kang

10 Norbulingka summer pavilion and park

11 The Drepung monastery

12 Statues carved in the cliff-face on the way to Lhasa

13 The Dalai Lama's throne

14 The author interviewing a barefoot doctor from the mountains

15 At the ante-natal clinic in a commune

16 and 17 At the carpet factory in Lhasa

18 Tibetan worker teaching a Han apprentice from Shanghai

19 A Tibetan blacksmith, now a delegate to the National Assembly

20 In a commune school

21 Two Tibetan boys dancing at the nursery of the *Lhasa Daily*

22 The Great Buddha brought from China by Princess Wen Cheng

23 Statues of the Nepalese wife of King Songtsang Kampo and his Chinese wife, Princess Wen Cheng

24 The author in a commune at Tsushui with Dr Shih from Shanghai (on left) and a Tibetan doctor and his wife

25 Jedi (second from left), Jen Yung (centre) and Tien Pao (second from right)

26 Medical tankas at the Menzekang

27 The author with Tien Pao

28 At the Drepung monastery with the lamas

29 The author in front of the Potala

barley yield had doubled, that wheat was expected to produce 'a double amount', by which is meant the same amount as the barley, in weight, and that all the communes wanted to follow 'the example of Tachai, in the inland'.

Because interviewing other farmers like Tzemu proved just as delightfully vague, I checked with officials—although this usually produces percentages. I found that grain production was now about 380 Chinese catties per mu, or about the same as north China and that was double what it was ten years ago. Overall total production of grain in Tibet had increased by round 49 per cent when compared with 1959. So Lhasa valley is slightly better off; but in southern Tibet (the Shan Nan region) model communes, such as Nyambad, or Lien Mai commune, known as the Tachai of Tibet produce much more, because they are diversifying into tea and rice.

In 1974 Tibet attained at last self-sufficiency in cereals. 'We have not had to import grain from inland this year.'

With Tzemu and other villagers, and a very handsome young man in a black gown, the director of the primary school (twenty-two years old), we walked to see the commune's pride, the 'new canal', a small, clear and rapid stream of water, pouring across the team's cultivated land. It was dug 'by all of us' said Tzemu. (But from what I saw, everywhere, more women than men were digging.) This water conservancy programme is going on all over Tibet. Very early one morning, round 5 a.m., I passed another village on the road north towards Tsinghai province, the yaks were still asleep. They moved when the headlights of our car discovered them. Women were up in the freezing pre-dawn, digging.

Red flags, banners, new trees—throughout the valley, 'New Tibet' say the villagers, 'we want a New Tibet.' Tsushui county, south of Lhasa, is an example of irrigation projects well thought out; but Tsushui is at the junction of the Kyi river with the Yalutsangpo; and there is abundant water and a hydro-electric plant; and here are tractors at work, in the fields. A whole village was tamping the sides of yet another

7

canal with bright new spades; they cheered as our car went by.

Although there are only 21,000 Tibetans in Tsushui county, in 35 communes, there are 102,800 yaks, cows, sheep and horses.[16] Cattle expansion has been slow since most of these are still privately owned, and the produce, except for wool, is 'for home consumption'. In the other agricultural communes, the proportion seems less, but a rough guess of 3 to 1, for all animals, is not amiss. In the high pastoral areas, of course, there are millions of sheep, yaks, and horses ...

On the road again, I notice a man coming back from Lhasa, a cavalier, stepping easily off his horse. Though buses ply the roads, horseback riding is still frequent. The man carries proudly a Thermos flask. He has purchased it in the supermarket in Lhasa. Unlike China, where every brigade has a shopping centre, and can support it because of its population, here it is still impossible; Tibetans will go on big jaunts, sometimes lasting days, to shop in the city, chiefly for Thermos flasks, plastics, cotton goods, and tennis shoes, and come back laden with the 'new goods'.

The Thermos flask and the pressure cooker are changing Tibetan life habits. Tsampa three times a day, tea with butter and barley, was the staple village diet. In the old days animal increase was kept to a minimum because meat was not bought or paid for; meat and animals were bartered for tea, wooden utensils, matches (a box of matches cost a sheep). The pastoral herdsmen ate meat abundant on the high plateaux, but in the valleys very little meat was consumed by the agricultural serfs, because their cattle were leased, and tribute was 60 to 70 per cent of the herd's output. Butter was in great part kept 'for the gods', to pay the lamas their tithe and levies, to pay for illness, divination or deaths.

Now with wheat flour, with money, diet is changing in the villages. Barley is still consumed, but tea, once expensive (a cow for 10 lbs of tea) is now not only cheap, it is being grown in southern Tibet itself. 'This is the principle of self-sufficiency in food. Tibet can and will produce all the food it needs, and more; the surplus can be sold and bring money for new development.' This principle is the one followed in every province of China; each one, in case of war, can and must sustain its own population in all essentials. This is also being done in Tibet.

Livestock has gone up in number by 30 per cent since 1959; but this has taken a great deal of doing, for the herds were decreasing. When veterinarian teams first started injecting the cattle against epidemics, the herdsmen refused; but when they saw cattle saved from epidemics (like rinderpest) then they believed.

There remains the problem of fuel: cow manure, gathered at home and burning slowly, is not efficient. There is talk of doing what I see being done in Szechuan, introducing methane gas from human manure, for cooking and heating water, which would be more efficient. And there are the coal mines now opened. But for some time yet, fuel for ordinary villages will be a problem.

Each commune has a school, a small clinic, a veterinary station, a savings fund, a cultural centre. Each is working on water canals, extending the area of the fields, saving money for mechanization. In each there are Tibetan cadres, young and not so young, persuading, teaching, exhorting—and working. For under the county administration, in the communes, all the cadres are 100 per cent Tibetan.

After three days, I realized that the plan for mechanization is not only possible but that it is the only way to speed up Tibet's emergence into the modern age. For although the population is increasing, and children no longer die, and there is no family planning, the Tibetan people cannot increase, in the next twenty-five years, to become what the country can easily support: at least twenty million, before it has enough manpower. This enormous region is potentially a huge granary; a great exporter of meat and milk products; it can become one of the wealthiest industrial areas in the world. It

has enormous resources of all kinds, including a vast potential
of hydro-electric power.

'We apply Chairman Mao's policies and line here. We must
materialize all these policies to make Tibet's economy progress
swiftly so that Tibet will become a wall of bronze, impregnable,
and the Tibetan people reach very rapidly the highest standards
of development and prosperity.'

I see tomatoes grow at 13,000 feet, and they are excellent
tomatoes. I have already mentioned the enormous cabbages,
drying pungently under my window. The soil in the valleys
can produce five times, ten times what it is producing today,
given a little fertilizer; but only machinery, tractors, harves-
ters, threshers, can solve the problem of population shortage.

Therefore, I am now convinced that it will be done, and far
quicker than one thinks.

In Tsushui county, I meet Tzejenchoma, thirty-six, head of the
women's federation, and Ishikesan, vice-chairman of the
county, also a woman. Here there are 71 cadres of Tibetan
nationality, of whom 32 are women cadres, mostly young. In
this county, and in Tetzin county, I visit the schools.

In Tsushui there are 3,800 children at school, or 82 per cent
of the total. The Tibetan average is 70 to 75 per cent of children
at school. These 3,800 children are in 55 primary schools, of
which 50 are in the 35 communes.

'There was learning only in the monasteries, for future
lamas; only nobles were taught, by tutors; religion mostly.
No science, no literature. Now we have 4,300 schools of the
primary type throughout Tibet. And of course, here again,
difficulties: where shall we get all the teachers needed for these
primary schools?'

In Sangmu commune, in Tetzin county, district of Tungka,
the school is typical; a very plain, small whitewashed building,
unpretentious, with a courtyard. It is divided into six rooms.
The children are in six classes, from eight to fourteen years of
age. They sit on the floor, and apart from the two higher

classes, write on their knees, on slates, with a small bit of wood dipped in soot and yak dung; they draw lines with a string rubbed with chalk and then pulled against the slate. In the last two classes there is paper to write on and textbooks. The textbooks are in Tibetan; all the teaching is in Tibetan. 'When they leave, they can read the newspaper, and they know also arithmetic, and a little science.'

The teachers are all very young, from 18 to 21. The headmaster is 22, and was the handsome youth in a black gown and elegant boots who accompanied me through the fields the other day. Graduates of the primary schools immediately become teachers; the headmaster himself only had two years' training at a secondary school before he came here. 'Lack of teachers is a big problem. Only the lamas, and not all of them, could read. We asked some of the lamas to help us. But it is difficult, they knew only prayers. And also the language has changed. They did not know the words for engine, electricity, motor, tractor ... atom, energy ... no words existed in Tibetan for the new things.'

The young headmaster is enthusiastic. His face glows with happiness as he shows me the children. Here there are 217 of them, 112 girls, and 105 boys. The textbooks are translations, in Tibetan, of textbooks used in Shanghai. 'And now we have paper, copybooks.' The headmaster, or one of the young teachers (they are all handsome, and all men – perhaps because Tibetan man is still the one who works less at manual labour than the woman does) goes to Lhasa to buy paper and books from the new printing press in Lhasa. 'There was no printing press before.'

Because I am, by nature, meticulous, I asked who funded this school. Very proudly, the young Tibetan headmaster told me that it was funded by the commune itself, with everyone contributing to the maintenance and upkeep; although the buildings had belonged to the serf-owner, and were granted without pay by the government.

I did some research. Stuart Gelder states that in 1962 there were already 1,300 primary schools in Tibet managed by the parents themselves. But most of these schools seem to have been in the towns, such as Lhasa (he did not, unfortunately, see any schools in the rural areas).

Since then, the additional 3,000 schools, to bring the number up to 4,300, are chiefly in rural areas. How many of these are funded by the communes themselves I am, at the moment, unable to say. But I should think that no more than a third are thus funded, because the schools in the pastoral areas are definitely government funded.

In 1962, when Gelder visited Tibet, thousands of lamas were coming out of the monasteries, and since many of them could read and write, they became the teachers in the new schools.

This information was vouchsafed to me spontaneously in the school I visited. 'We had also at the beginning ex-lamas for teachers; and they did all they could. But there were many difficulties; since there was a great deal they did not know.' They could teach reading, writing, and primary arithmetic. Also dancing and singing. But at the moment, the problem is to train teachers in science, in technology, in all that makes the twentieth century possible. And therefore the source of teaching, represented by the ex-lamas, is no longer a possibility; for they are clearly marked by their own upbringing in the monasteries.

In the rural commune schools, the Han language is not taught, only Tibetan. 'This produces a difficulty, if the children go up for secondary education in the sciences.' I would find out later how this difficulty is to be managed.

Of course paper and textbooks are free. No workpoints are allotted if a child is withdrawn from school to work, which used to happen. 'We do not want the children to be taken out of school before they have finished their primary education, at fourteen or fifteen.'

Once again it is evening; I hear the women singing, returning with their spades and hoes from digging the canal. Their bright aprons and head cloths glow in the light of the sinking sun. The young headmaster and I walk through cold blue shadows to the road. There, carved in the cliff is a large coloured Buddha of stone. And suddenly a small pig appears from nowhere, jumping and hopping, going home.

'It is our Tibetan pig,' says the headmaster. 'It jumps over walls. Our Han brothers are helping us to crossbreed with a larger pig; then we shall also learn to have piggeries, for fertilizer.'

'The pig is an admirable animal,' I reply, 'it produces three tons of fertilizer a year, besides meat, leather, bristles.'

Talking of pigs and fertilizers, we take our leave. Tibet's first fertilizer factory has just gone into operation, in Chamdo. It will produce 3,000 tons of chemical fertilizer a year. 'But we shall also have our own, here, one day ... we want to have factories here too ... my brother is working in a factory that has just opened, in the south ... '

We hurry back to Lhasa before night falls, because it suddenly gets freezingly cold and Dr Ma is solicitous, afraid that 'the old lady' (that is me) will catch a cold. And in Lhasa, it is very dangerous to have a cold; it may turn into bronchitis within hours. Tomorrow I investigate the clinics, the hospitals, the health services. But there are many questions in my mind. Where will the machines come from for mechanization? Where will the people who run machines come from? Where are the Tibetan agronomists being trained now? So much to know, and all the problems inter-related. There, above the road, looms the Potala, which I am beginning to dislike. Night spread a banquet of stars; stars so large, so heavy, they look like flowers ready to drop into my hands.

5

The New Magic of Medicine

Impiety was the dreaded sin of Tibetans; far worse than plague. The prayer wheel to ward off demons, and bring merit, was the most common object seen; even herdsmen guarding their masters' sheep, or playing games,[1] passed a prayer wheel around to keep it going during any activity. I have only seen one prayer wheel, in the hand of a small old lady, who sits on the sidewalk of Lhasa's broad leafy avenue surrounded by charming Pekinese dogs (nine of them). Impiety was implicit in any new medical care; immunizing cattle against disease; rounding up the mad stray dogs; vaccination and inoculations. Even when Tibetan students were trained in veterinarian or medical work, they prayed hard, at night, to be forgiven for their sins of the day.[2]

But now the word impiety is not heard. I meet Dr Tzejen Choka, who is thirty-three years old, a robust, dark-faced woman, once a slave, now vice-director of the public health service for all Tibet. She led a delegation to the World Health Organization in Geneva in the spring of 1975. She and I spent some days together, visiting clinics and hospitals and talking of health measures.

'Education out of superstition—bedrock of ignorance and conservatism' is not easy. And here the Tibetan woman proves a main factor for change. For it is upon her that the goal—increase of population, and a healthy population—depends. All begins with birth; birth in cow byres, in stables, is not precisely a good start. Persuading women to give birth in the house is not feasible, since 'houses' are one large room; since there is no change of clothing, nor are there sheets or blankets. The rough, homespun wool robe was worn day and night, year after year, and never washed (nor was the body under it). It also acted as bedding at night. Herdsmen-serfs had no shoes or boots; they and their women and children walked in the snow bare-footed. The weak succumbed quickly, for the mother rolled her newborn in snow—and if it died, that was the will of the gods. Tuberculosis, due to the dark and foul interior of houses, and also due to infected milk was rife and is still frequent. Every week, cases of tuberculous meningitis in children are received at the General Hospital in Lhasa, which started as a small outpatient clinic, under tents, in 1951.

Although on the whole there is no protein deficiency in Tibet, due to butter, milk and some meat (sun dried), there is much intestinal disease of all types, including parasites, since there is no proper cooking; water boils here at 70 degrees centigrade, so that plunging one's hand in a pan of boiling water does not scald. Changes in food habits, in toilet habits, in washing habits, all these involve educating the women.

Smallpox and venereal disease were wiped out; the incidence rate of the latter according to some reports, was near 80 per cent of the adult population. The Hans keep quiet about it, not wishing to offend 'our Tibetan brothers'. But the true orientation of medical care, with 'priority for the rural areas' only began during the Cultural Revolution. 'Before that work was hampered by the wrong line of the capitalist-roaders in the Party, who only cared about health in the cities, and doctors and hospitals in the cities.'[3] In 1959, there were 200 hospital beds in the whole of Tibet and only in Lhasa, and Chamdo. In 1975, there were 3,800 and of these 80 per cent below county level or at county level, in the rural areas.

'Our programme for public health must be thought out in conjunction with the policy for agricultural development,' said Dr Tzejen Choka. 60 per cent of all funds granted by the Central Government (in 1975 twelve times the amount that was given in 1965) are devoted to the countryside health services. 60 per cent of the medical personnel of Tibet is in rural areas; and 30 per cent of the city personnel of hospitals and clinics must, every year, rotate in teams in the rural areas. Added to this are comprehensive medical teams, 100 to 200 strong, come from city hospitals in China. They choose a remote area, where they stay for two years, establishing medical research centres and clinics, overhauling the local medical personnel, training new recruits, 'some of our best health services are not in the cities, but in the more remote border areas'. It is evident that all this would not be possible had not roads been built; and food assured by the PLA starting State farms, to feed themselves and the influx of technical and scientific personnel sent from China to start industry and hospitals and schools. Supplies are assured by the convoys of lorries that ply the roads, day and night, with their maintenance teams, and small road hostels, and petrol dumps, along these 16,000 kilometres built since 1950.

Not only is modern medical care emphatic on prevention – available in each village, and even on the pastoral plateaux – but a great effort is being made to resurrect Tibetan medicine, to unwrap it from its smother of witchcraft, magic, exorcisms, cabalistic ritual and astrology, to study it scientifically and to use it. This again follows the Mao line: that there should be alliance between Chinese and Western medicine, using the scientific study techniques of the latter to understand, improve, and use the former. Here, in New Tibet, the formula is: 'Triple alliance between Han, Tibetan and Western medicine.'

We visit the Menzekang Tibetan hospital, created by the thirteenth Dalai Lama in 1915. It is one of the only two medical centres which existed in Old Tibet. On Iron Hill is the abandoned building of the Medical College, said to have been founded two or three hundred years ago. In 1959 Iron Hill was one of the strongholds of the conspirators, and the old Medical College was also invested. It has remained preserved by the sun and buffeted by the wind, but there are no longer any lamas there.

It was in this old college that monks were trained in medicine, with astrology and divination. From here lamas blew into great horns, three times a month, and also when the wind — the wind in Tibet is a maelstrom of dust and sand — snuffed out the sky and the sun. 500 monks in 1955-6 took care of the prelates, nobles, and the army officers; although a small horde of unqualified lamas properly exercised, upon the serfs, their monopoly of exorcism and prayer. Not counting the temples, where the sick went with butter and supplication to the serene deities on their thrones of gold. No patients were ever seen at the Iron Hill College. They were seen at the Menzekang.

It was those holy men who taught that twins were the product of a coupling with a malefic spirit. Twins were abandoned to die, or sometimes burnt alive with their 'witch-mother', especially in rural areas.

The Menzekang is a small, flat-roofed structure bright with new whitewash. Its large entrance courtyard is filled with patients and their families — for the whole family comes with the sick man or woman or child, so that in the new hospitals provision must be made for them. Here are herdsmen in sheepskin with fur caps; women with pigtails wound with coloured ribbons and bulky black gowns relieved by the usual striped apron; they look more like strollers than patients, and I am told that 'there are sometimes around one thousand patients a day', which obviously shows that many people still cling to Tibetan remedies — as in China, where in every hospital the patient is given a choice between Chinese or western-type consultations.

I meet, in the large hall of the Menzekang, eighteen Tibetan doctors, of whom seven are above forty. There are three young women doctors, again a breakthrough and an innovation. The doctors vary greatly in appearance; some have the aquiline features denoting Arab stock; others are more flat-faced with high Mongolian cheekbones. Some wear a Muslim cap on their heads. It confirms what the observant Père Huc wrote in

1846; that it was the Muslims in Tibet who maintained a medical tradition. In fact, the Menzekang was sometimes in conflict with the lamas of the school of medicine, though astrology, religion, and exorcism were to win in the end.

Today the Menzekang is expanding. Backed by government loans, helped by a medical research team, it is establishing its own hospital beds, around twenty of them; and a research group with young trainees. A comprehensive study of the value of Tibetan traditional remedies is taking place.

Tibetan medicine is derived from Chinese medicine, so I am told; and also that it was almost 2,000 years old; but Tibetans are very vague about dates. Again Songtsang Kampo the seventh-century King, and Princess Wen Cheng his spouse, and Princess Tsing Cheng who came fifty years later (A.D. 710) are invoked; the ladies brought medical men and copies of the Chinese medical encyclopedia and other books. Moxibustion, herbal remedies are from China; but acupuncture is absent, probably because it was 'impiety' to make a hole in the body. Although it was perfectly admissible to main a man, cutting off hand or foot; a curious paradox. Religion also stopped the dissection of bodies, and surgery, which apparently was performed around 1,200 years ago.

Dr Maimayishi, aged forty-seven, twenty-two years a doctor, tells me that when he saw the lamas in the 1950s crowding the first clinic established in Lhasa (which has now become the General Hospital) for penicillin shots, he was also converted to studying 'other types of medicine'. It took fifteen years to become a 'doctor-lama', of which nine or ten were devoted to memorizing the four canons of Tibetan medicine, written by Youtoyundenkungpo (also spelt Udoyongden Gambo) at the time of the Greath Fifth. There was the taking of the six pulses, and looking at the colour of the tongue, the eyes, the skin, the urine and excreta.

Tutandzejen, sixty-eight, a doctor for forty-five years is heavily pockmarked, but a specialist in bronchitis and respiratory diseases – common and killing in Tibet. He is also a member of the research team, studying arterio-sclerotic changes and the effect of Tibetan herbs upon them. Kungkopingsa, aged seventy, is a distinguished man, fine-featured with a small silky white beard. He was a lama 'when I was fourteen', and studied at the Iron Hill School of Medicine. 'I studied astronomy and astrology too.' He is a specialist in stomach ulcers. He tells me that some herbs must be taken at dawn; others when the dew is leaving the ground; and it all depends on the moon and the stars. I ask him: 'Which is better, the old or the new?' He replies diplomatically: 'We now have the best of both worlds.'

We go back to the topic of surgery. It seems that 1,200 years ago dissection and operations were practised by Tengzenlobu, who left anatomical charts, and drawings of the surgical instruments he used. But because 'some people died after operations', religion forbade any surgery. It does seem strange that in a land where 'heavenly burial' occurs, where the body is dissected by professional undertakers, there should have been continued ignorance of human organs; for the canons say the heart of woman is on the right, that of man on the left, and circulation begins in the right hand. But this dogmatism also occurred in medieval Europe.

Winnington and Gelder were shown marvellously inaccurate drawings of the body organs. But I saw, hanging on the wall, a series of tankas—those paintings on silk, framed in rich brocade—of which one represented an accurate dissection of the human male, back and front, and four more the animal, mineral and vegetable components from which remedies are made. Horns of bull and mountain goat and deer and rhinoceros, musk glands and spleen and gall bladder of various beasts and snakes and birds; shells of snails, but no fish. (Fish is plentiful in the Yalutsangpo river but is never eaten in Tibet.) I ask why the anatomical chart seems so accurate, when those seen by my predecessors in Lhasa were highly inaccurate. There are eighty-eight such charts, they tell me; this one, which is very old, is accurate, hence it was hung up. But no one really knows when it was painted.

We pass into other rooms, filled with burlap bags containing pills, herbs and powders. Tibetan herbs are not boiled in a decoction to be drunk, as in China; they are ground, together with the animal and mineral ingredients, into pills, orange and brown and black.

According to Dr Chantim, twenty-eight, under-secretary of the revolutionary committee of the Menzekang, there were only two doctors here before 1959; one to diagnose the disease and prescribe; the other to record. Seven aides to distribute pills or prepare them. And no beds.

I also visit the factory for making Tibetan pills; here everything is ground into powder by something resembling a flour mill, activated by electricity (there is a power station in Lhasa, expanded from the very small one which functioned only four hours a day before 1959).

I look at the patients lying in beds in a clean room in an adjoining building; this is the new expansion of the Menzekang. Apparently Tibetan remedies against rheumatoid arthritis are very effective; also against epilepsy, and chronic inflammatory diseases and nephritis. Since last year ulcers (also very frequent, as are intestinal diseases and parasites) are detected by X-ray, but now cured with Tibetan herbs. There are 80 different kinds of medicines of local source now being tried here, and the total number of personnel is nearly 100, but 'will increase to 200 pretty soon'. 61,000 lbs of medicines of Tibetan origin were compounded in 1974, versus 300 lbs in 1965.

In Lhasa too is the modern General Hospital; brick buildings in wide grounds with trees, vegetable plots and flower pots. Its beginnings, under tents, as outpatient clinic only, were difficult due to religious hostility. But it is now established, with a mixed staff of Han and Tibetan personnel. Here in the outpatients there is a vast crowd; and what a difference! For whereas at the Menzekang they look more like people come to Lhasa for a visit, here are the really sick; on stretchers, lying on the floor; others against the wall, very pale, some skeletal looking; and as usual relatives and children crowd about.

There is a very strong odour too. It is probable that sick people go first to the Menzekang, and only come here when all else has failed ...

The hospital is frightfully busy, and obviously will have to expand, enlarge, aggrandize. Between two operations the surgeon, Dr Yu, and Dr Tung, hospital director and head of the department of internal medicine, come to speak with me; but I know that patients are waiting and so we gallop through, talking medicine in terse, shorthand sentences, since no interpreter is needed, both are Hans. No time for ornate speeches, or even for a cup of tea. As a physician myself, I am caught by the efficiency, the excellent, painstaking, and thorough work of nurses and doctors here. It is by no means a luxurious place, gleaming with chrome and paint. It is adequate, and the wonderful personnel, many of them Tibetans, are using the limited facilities to the fullest extent. There are modern operating theatres, X-ray rooms, laboratories. The beds are functional, and all are full in the wards we skim through, and among the children are many cases of pneumonia. But there is always an attentive nurse doing what is necessary. It is not easy, for many beds are surrounded with relatives and parents in odorous homespun and boots, but the good temper, and trust and human care and devotion about this hospital are inspiring, and I am passed from doctor to doctor, and spend two hours examining everything, including the blood bank, for which many Han cadres and PLA contribute blood 'and now our Tibetan brothers and sisters are also enthusiastic, they are no longer afraid'. But of course it is the Tibetan cadres, the general population is not yet quite up to it. A new brain surgery unit is going to be opened; a Shanghai medical team is here, for research, and will fan out to the plateaux soon.

The hospital has only 250 beds; it needs 400 by next year, 'although now, with the net of hospitals and clinics in rural areas, we shall probably have less work'. Dr Lin, the competent obstetrician shows me the maternity wards and the babies' room. There are three incubators for premature babies and a pair of twins, alive, in two of them. 'We do much teaching of the mothers and they now come to hospitals to have the baby.' But of course, those are mostly Lhasa city people, although there are also emergency cases sent in by ambulance from 100 kilometres around, and Caesareans are 'fairly frequent' especially in winter. I wonder how many twins are still regarded as devil's seed. Later I shall meet a Tibetan woman, now a cadre, who saw her mother burnt alive with the triplets she had borne.

Here also are students and paramedical personnel; Tibetans from the secondary schools in Lhasa and other cities, barefoot doctors from the villages, and workers from the new factories, come here in batches to do three or four months' practical work at the General Hospital. They learn 'on the spot', help the nurses, learn cleanliness and how to sterilize instruments and simple techniques. There is also a nursing school in Lindze, a new industrial town on the Yalutsangpo, south of Lhasa (400 kilometres), and the training of Tibetan midwives is also done there.

Dr Yu has time to tell me that the complexion of disease is changing in Tibet, as it has done in China. More cancer cases, unfortunately usually in the terminal stages. No more epidemics, still some tertiary syphilis. Both he and Dr Tung have been here twelve and fourteen years respectively. They have the dark faces and purplish cheekbones of Tibetans, due to the increase in red blood cells to cope with the rarefied oxygen. In fact, when they go back home in north China on holidays, everyone thinks they are genuine Tibetans! I observe this among the Hans who have been here some years, they look Tibetan.

The last few minutes are given to Dr Chomayangtsung, thirty-six, and Hsiachin, a barefoot Memba trainee of twenty-one, who are both in charge of family planning ... for Tibetan women cadres in Lhasa. Although family planning is not encouraged the Tibetan women cadres, doctors, administrators, teachers are a considerable number in Tibet, 12,000 out of 27,000; they are educated, married; most of them have three or four children, and do not want any more. So there is this small room to teach family planning, but only on demand. 'There is a contradiction between woman's liberation, her blossoming and participation in study and work, and having many children. On the other hand, we must let our Tibetan sisters decide themselves.' And so a Tibetan woman doctor for Tibetan women, and everything left to individual decision.

'Medicine must go to the people, not wait for the people to come to the hospital.' Although this is not a teaching hospital; it does teach, especially for the rural para-medical personnel. Dr Tung's last sentences as he shakes hands are about altitude sickness; research is going on. Han children from the lowlands do badly here, many suffer from altitude sickness; I have seen one, in his mother's arms in a ward. He is going by the plane tomorrow morning. 'This is not an acute case.' In acute cases, oxygen in large quantities is available; there is now an oxygen factory in Lhasa.

Back into the countryside, flooded with sun; Dr Tzejen Choka takes me now southwards to Tsushui county again, to see the county hospital. Every one of the seventy-three counties has a small hospital, every district a clinic; every commune a health station. Medical books in Tibetan are printed and distributed; they are in the style of those given to the barefoot doctors in other regions of China.

In Tibet, too, there are now barefoot doctors. As in China, they are young people (the age limit between seventeen and twenty-eight), the sons and daughters of serfs and slaves, and they are 'not divorced from labour'. They plant and plough and hoe, but also administer preventive inoculations and every production team, which is the village, has at least one. The General Hospital in Lhasa and the county hospitals maintain close links with exchanges of doctors (one-third of the Lhasa hospital doctors are in rural areas, rotating every six to nine months). The doctors from the county hospital 'go down' to inspect the district clinics and the health stations in the communes. From those young barefoot doctors are sent to the city hospital to train for some months.

Tsushui county hospital has electricity; a hydro-electric power station has been built, and is now being expanded, for new industries are coming here. Already I see a cement factory along the road, surrounded by *rice* fields cultivated by the workers who are chiefly Han, although some Tibetan workers are also gradually coming. The principle is the same: every factory must feed itself, and also have its own health clinic. The county hospital is therefore small, a typical adobe, flat-roofed collection of village type, but with glass windows and twenty beds, (population 21,000 in the county), and the capacity to add ten or fifteen more 'if necessary'. Dr Shih from Shanghai, is in charge; his aide is a Tibetan doctor, Ishikesan, again a former slave, whose mother had thirteen children, most of whom died in infancy; whose father was brutalized and beaten by the lord and died of it.

Tsushui county is a model in health; Dr Shih tells me that preventive inoculations in Tibet cover 'round 80 per cent of the children' and one district, Tzeman, has covered 100 per cent. This year there have been no deaths from measles, also a killer due to bronchitis — 'we have worked ourselves into a state of unemployment,' says slim, cheerful Dr Shih, showing me there are only six patients in the twenty-bed hospital. But then this is harvest time, when hospital attendance falls off very greatly. Dr Shih is from Shanghai but is burnt mahogany by the sun; only when he lifts his long sleeve can one see that his skin is white. In Tsushui county investigation has revealed that gonorrhoea has disappeared, as it has in Nachu county further south. But Dr Shih is modest; he says that his work 'is still very deficient', and praises another county, Gyantze, which has 8 districts, 43 communes, 233 production teams and 41,000 people (again the same average of less than 1,000 per commune), of whom 21,000 are women; of these 21,000, 12,000 are over 16 years old and 'of child-bearing age'. There is a mid-wife there, Pasang Tzuchen, who is 30, whose mother gave birth to twins and was killed with the twins. After liberation Pasang Tzuchen became literate, became a revolutionary, and a midwife, and now has organized the women there, has started a midwifery and 'middle medical technique' (para-medical) school, and is equipping nurseries. 'We in Tsushui are trying to do the same.' The population growth, Dr Shih estimates, is now between 2 or 2·5 per cent, depending on the regions, in Tibet.[4] The lowest is still in the high pastoral plateaux of Ali, where there is only 'one family every 10 square kilometres, or even less than that'. To help the Tibetan woman who is 'a most important labour power' by tradition, and yet to fulfil the wish for many healthy children and popu-lation increase, antenatal clinics, maternity care, child care, nurseries are emphasized in the programme for health in the countryside. It is the county hospital which is the active nucleus for deploying these medical plans.

'We must educate, but also wait for awareness. There must be no commandism,' says Dr Tzejen Choka.

'At the beginning, there was mutual ignorance; our Tibetan brothers knew nothing about us; we knew nothing about them,' says Dr Shih. 'The lamas prevented the rural people from coming, especially the women ... '

Because distances are so great, transport is a difficulty; there is a county ambulance, but horses and PLA jeeps are also a great help. 'Every hospital has its horses,' says Dr Shih. 'And every doctor must learn to ride.'

Dr Shih shows me the X-ray apparatus. The antenatal clinic is full of visiting mothers-to-be, a gratifying sight. The out-patient registration department is divided into three; those who seek 'Tibetan medical care', those who seek 'Han medicine', or 'western-type medicine'.

The clinic of the district of Tzeman has three 'barefoot doctors'. Two of them are sturdy village girls of eighteen and nineteen. The third, a boy, is out on a visit. Tzeman district which has the best record of preventive inoculation of all the county has also, as many areas of Tibet, more women than men.[5]

The clinic is one small whitewashed room, with a white curtain dividing it in two, hiding a bed for examination of the patient. The girls smile and show me their simple equipment; first aid; but everything is clean and well kept, and in the drug cupboard everything is labelled in both Han and Tibetan. The county also has six midwives. Altogether, there have been 20,000 'cases seen' of all kinds this year (1975), for a population of 21,000 in the country, not a bad record.

In another county, Tetsin, nearer Lhasa and with 27,000 people, I also visit the clinics, the antenatal one where a very cheerful young woman doctor from Shanghai is seeing patients. She has learnt Tibetan and does not need an interpreter. 'We all try to learn the language.' There are 110 barefoot doctors and medical personnel in the county. But Dr Tzejen Choka insists that the more remote the commune from the county town or the hospital, the better the medical care, and the more barefoot doctors allotted. Unfortunately it would take a week in a lorry to go to a 'really remote place'. 'Self-reliance' in medical care is now the theme, an effort to organize clinics 'with the masses', that is, with the barefoot doctors and the Tibetans themselves starting them voluntarily. A barefoot doctor is paid a very small stipend (about nine yuan a month) by the government but is supposed to get work points like any other working peasant. The average works out at 240 days' 'labour' a year, and the other 120 days' 'medical work' are covered by the stipend, with extra work points allotted for them. 'Some of our barefoot doctors in pastoral areas travel one to two days on horseback to go and see a patient—that must count as labour.'

Since tetanus which once was rife has now been controlled, the highest mortality among village babies is now from dysentery and diarrhoea. 'This means changing food habits.' This is also related to improving cattle, since bovine tuberculosis is a cause of morbidity and mortality, and cooking habits must change. 'There is still a great deal of education to do,' sighs Dr Shih. But already women are coming to the county hospital to deliver; they find it so practical. And the midwives try to educate the woman, to prevent manure getting on to the navel of the newborn; and all this also depends on the new canals being dug, on the supply of clean water. For Tibetans, like medieval Europeans, do not wash.

Returning to Lhasa, we stop on the road by the exhibition hall, where a conference has grouped 500 barefoot doctors from all over Tibet, for discussion of the topic: 'Health work oriented towards the fulfilment of the agricultural programme'. The hall's main room is filled with exhibits of plants, and minerals, collected by the barefoot doctors themselves, neatly labelled according to area.[6] Among the 300-odd specimens on exhibition, some are fossil snails, and sea shells, which are also pounded into medicine and are sovereign remedies, it is said, for certain diseases. The fossils, hewn with their containing rock, are several million years old; they date from when Tibet was a great sea, before the earth's convulsions thrust it way up in the air, before the Himalayas—geologically speaking, young mountains—were born.

I meet around twenty barefoot doctors, young men and women, dressed in the various garbs of their regions, some come from Ali, and others from near the Aksai Chin, and yet others from the border with Burma. Stolid, sturdy people, they grinned and pressed round without any shyness. One of them, a young man of twenty-four, had an opaque, blind eye. He came from a high valley in the Karakorum. When I asked what had happened to his eye, he would not tell me, but Dr Tzejen Choka did. The young man was riding from family to family (and there the herdsmen still live under felt tents) giving inoculations to the children. He had been so busy that when a small ampoule containing serum he was filing broke and one piece of glass got into his eye he had had no time to look after himself, nor did he seek any help for his own eye because he wanted to finish his task first. Thus he lost one eye.

There are 6,400 barefoot doctors in Tibet, all of them Tibetans; 1,300 youths from secondary schools are being trained in medical knowledge in various institutes, and also in Lhasa, to become barefoot doctors. 'We plan to involve six per thousand of the population thoroughly in health care, educating them so that they will educate the others.'

And so the apparatus of magic and terror, where all was explained by demons, and supplication and incantation is now gone. Perhaps that is why I only saw one prayer wheel in Tibet.

6

The Birth of the Worker—New Lhasa

There was no industry of any kind in Tibet. Nor was crafts-
manship honoured as in certain pre-industrial countries. Like
the Nepalese, Tibetan woodcarvers and craftsmen in jewellery
were excellent; but all this art and talent went to the temples,
to the nobles. Lhasa, the parasite city, lived off religious objects
and luxury goods imported from India, selling to the more
wealthy pilgrims. One of the main items of consumption, tea,
had to be imported (on the backs of men and yaks). There was
no light industry; cloth for the serfs was homewoven, rough,
and lived in till it dropped with dirt. For the nobles, silk and
brocades were imported from China, and very fine wool cloth,
pulu, was produced by the weavers of Lhasa and Shigatze and
Gyantze for their robes.[1] Swiss watches, cameras, and French
perfume, imported from India on yak's back, sewn into bags
of hide, tins of Australian butter (in a place which burnt a ton
of butter a day to the gods!) were sold in Lhasa at high prices.
The distortion in trade introduced, not only by the British
'treaties' of the early twentieth century, but also by the fact
that trade was in the hands of lamas and nobles, and by the
general poverty of the population, made it impossible for
native production to flourish, except in such items as were
necessary to support the religious aspect of Lhasa the Holy
City; the adorning of temples, of noble houses, and of monasteries; the demands of pilgrims for ex-votos and objects of
piety, or gold, to be lavished upon the temples.

'Tibetan aristocrats and leading monks are the biggest
traders,' wrote Winnington. Tibetan society allowed no 'third

estate' to develop as rival to the dominance of the church and gentry, but absorbed the merchants into that unique creation ... the monk, noble, official and merchant embodied in a single person. As a result, every monastery – and each one, having its power to levy taxes, was a state within a state – had its own trading network. The primitive organization, lack of roads and costliness of transport, made trade highly profitable only to the '626' real masters of Tibet. And it made all manufactured goods, even the simplest, highly expensive, out of reach for the 90 per cent or more of serfs.

One of the grievances of the monasteries against the Hans when they came was that, with the roads, and the introduction of light industrial goods at cheap prices, and also the cutting off of smuggling from India, 'trade' became far less possible for them, even if the State trading company, to avoid market dislocation, sold only wholesale. Prices went down. Tea was already 30 per cent cheaper when the road reached Lhasa in 1954. And matches were now obtainable for 2 lbs of raw untreated wool, instead of paying one whole sheep.

But the essence of the reforms, agreed to by the Panchen Lama and Dalai Lama in March 1955 ('the road for Tibet is the road of socialism' the Dalai Lama stated) was the industrialization of Tibet itself, using its resources, unused or wasted, to build its own people's prosperity.

Today, there are 252 'small and medium' industries implanted in Tibet; some began in 1959, but most of them began after 1965, during and after the Cultural Revolution. Industrialization is thought out in terms of the autonomy of the region; just as self-sufficiency in food is also a part of the autonomy. In a sense, each province in China practises this self-reliant economy, developing its own resources and becoming as self-sufficient as possible in food, so that in case of war each will be able to sustain its people in essentials, and not be subordinate or dependent upon other regions or provinces. If Tibet's autonomy was to be true autonomy, industrialization and enhanced agricultural production must be its foundation.

And the preparatory committee for Tibet's autonomy embodied the propositions for this development, by the Tibetans themselves.

The Dalai Lama's subsequent charges that 'there was plenty of food and shortage was unknown' only refers to his own class, the 200 families. The charge that the Hans extorted food and thus provoked shortages is absurd. The Han Chinese do not eat milk, butter and barley tsampa. Every PLA unit started growing, on unused land (95 per cent of potentially cultivable land was unused), their own food and keeping their own pigs. Twelve such State farms are in existence today, of which three are in the Chamdo area.

At least forty rich mineral deposits—including gold and bauxite and titanium and silver and iron; arsenic and borax and mica and manganese; copper and lead and zinc and molybdenum; antimony and salt and sulphur, barytes, graphite, jade and uranium ... and most recently, oil—were discovered in Tibet by geological survey teams between 1955 and 1975. And twenty million tons of coal very near to Lhasa itself, as well as several deposits in Chamdo. But mining was impiety, it annoyed the gods of the earth; only gold washed from the rivers was allowed, and all of it went to cover the tombs and the statues, the roofs of the monasteries, temples, sanctuaries, and palaces. Any industry, as well as mining for minerals, also confronted some taboo or other. Conversations carried out by that very perceptive man, Alan Winnington, with ministers and officials in 1955 showed 'the terrific mental conflict apparent as soon as any discussion with Tibetans goes below the surface' and came to grips with the concrete proposals of reform and of industrialization in Tibet.[2]

The tanning and preparing of hides for leather by machinery, the use of the abundant wool, the tinning of milk and meat—all of these light industrial processes would be hampered by religious interdictions. Despite fulsome speeches, the reality was obstruction.[3] Besides the immediately popular medical teams (of which lamas and nobles, despite 'impiety' also availed

themselves when ill), the only industrial improvements before
1959 were the reinforcing of the very small hydro-electric
power station in Lhasa (begun by the British), some minor
changes in spinning and weaving for rugs, an electric power
station at Shigatze, the roads built by the PLA, and some work
on river control, to prevent the flooding of Lhasa and Shigatze.
After 1959 industrialization began, but its debut was slow.

One of the most successful industries implanted was the
comprehensive wool and textile factory at Lindze (also spelt
Nyingchi). This modern factory had to wait first for a hydro-
electric power station to be installed on the Yalutsangpo river,
which flows through the area. There the water flows down-
wards on its journey to the plains of India and power is plentiful. The factory was imported, every piece of equipment for it,
and also around 12,000 workers and 1,000 administrative personnel and other staff, by lorries, all the way from Shanghai,
where it was sited, a distance of 5,000 kilometres; in itself a
stunning feat. Previously a great deal of the wool in Tibet from
the five million sheep (now doubled in number) was totally
wasted. Native artisans could only spin one quarter of the wool
available; the serfs never could buy any clothing; crude wool
was exported by yak's back to India and Kashmir; the finest
and best would make the pulu, for the wine-dark robes of the
prelates. Due to lack of transport, only around one half of the
wool, if that, ever got sold or used. The factory at Lindze
solved the problem of utilization of wool, and immediately
monetarized the pastoral serfs. Lhasa and Gyantze hand-made
Tibetan rugs were famous but scarce. Carpets were made at
home, by weavers using hand bobbins, spinning carpet yarn
by hand; dyeing was done elsewhere; and the rugs went to the
lama-traders, some for export to India, others for the houses of
nobles and the monasteries.

Hence the Potala, filled with sumptuous Tibetan rugs. The
craftsmen worked for the big monasteries and the nobles without pay, for ula; lived on what they sold to the pilgrims or to
private customers or traders. Shoemakers received a handful of

barley flour, and very little money, for making boots for the army, which occupied them two months a year. They made boots for nobles and lamas without pay, while herdsmen-serfs had no boots at all, and walked barefoot in the snow. The same with wood-turners. 'Whatever the temples ordered had to be made free of charge.'

Even the small changes made before 1959, such as introducing some spinning wheels and foot-treadles were 'impiety' and artisans were forbidden by the lamas to enter 'factories', even if these were only primitive cooperatives with some simple machinery. And craftsmen had to pay taxes for *not* doing *corvée*, and also their wives and daughters. Women had to pay in general more taxes than men if they remained 'unemployed', not doing *corvée*.

The wool factory in Lindze was at first manned by Han workers, who began by tilling the fields around the factory to provide food for themselves. A whole system of transport for the wool from the plateaux was dependent on roads being built. By 1959, the road builders had reached the western plateaux of Tibet with a main trunk road, and wool could then be transported by subsidiary roads.[4]

Leather factories to make boots and shoes came into being. They too would not have been possible, nor would the system whereby young 'apprentices' stamped the leather, by foot, in acid solutions (which grievously burnt their legs and feet) have been changed, without the installation of machinery to treat the hides.

The notion of wages and of working in factories for wages, was already being instilled in the Tibetans by 1959. Now, through industrialization a new class, the worker class, unknown in Tibet before, would be born.

'We are the new proletariat of New Tibet! We are the first generation of the working class of Tibet!'

I am visiting the motor vehicle maintenance and repair factory in Lhasa.

And here I see new Lhasa.

There are two Lhasas; the old, much shorn of its former bustle, since Lhasa is no longer a pilgrimage city. The shops are now cooperatives of artisans and craftsmen; their livelihood is assured, they no longer depend on lords and prelates. They produce for cooperatives which assure the transport and the selling of their goods. Old crafts are retained; at the Canton fair and in Hong Kong one finds new Tibetan products: rugs, ornate turquoise and silver-gilt boxes and animals, turquoise and coral necklaces, and pendants and wrist bangles; once made entirely for the monasteries and the nobility. Tibet now derives an income from these handicrafts which sustains the artisans of Lhasa, Shigatze, Gyantze.

But new Lhasa is something quite different. Lhasa is now a municipality; comprising not only the city, in which, I am told, there is a 40,000-strong population of fixed inhabitants but also a much larger area surrounding the old city and another area of communes among which small industries are growing, which extends eastwards,[5] and whose total population is 100,000 people. There are altogether twenty-eight factories in this greater Lhasa, not very large, but then the policy—as in China—is not to introduce large industrial complexes which will subordinate other areas to its needs; but to 'spawn' as swiftly as possible a multitude of small and medium factories, to develop each locality, and especially to serve the growing needs for consumer goods of the rural population. In 'Old Tibet', fully a quarter of Lhasa's population were beggars, living off the pilgrims' piety, grovelling in enormous garbage piles for shelter. But even the beggars have now entered factories, and become 'Tibet's first generation of workers', as my enquiries would discover.

The vehicle maintenance and repair factory of Lhasa is unimpressive to look at, but sprawls over a fairly large area, since land is the most abundant thing in Tibet. The workshops and living quarters are widely spaced; already construction on the same site of new, larger buildings goes on.

I am met by members of the factory revolutionary committee; four of them Tibetans, of whom two are women, and
four Hans.

This factory is part of the transport department, the road
maintenance system established by the PLA. This is one of the
main plants since new Lhasa is the hub of a network of roads.
There are ninety roads, big and small, radiating from it. The
factory started its essential work in 1957, and is placed under
the State Council of the Central Government.

The briefing with the revolutionary committee is short; no
prepared speeches, no reading out of prepared notes. Everything pours out, good naturedly, with much laughter. Questions are answered immediately; and the Hans do not speak
except, occasionally, when asked. Out of the four Tibetans,
three speak adequate Han. 'The Tibetans learn a language very
quickly, they are most intelligent. It takes them only nine
months to speak fairly good Han.' The good feeling, friendli-
ness and trust as all sit familiarly round, no one 'higher or
lower' is very striking. Especially to me, because in some parts
of China, before the Cultural Revolution, I saw bureaucratism
establish a hierarchy and no one spoke except the Party Secretary—something which Chairman Mao himself denounced.
Here, also, Tibetan women will sit with their male colleagues,
there is not the bunching together of the women, relic of
Confucian prudery, which I still find for instance in north
China.

'In 1957, when we began, the Szechuan–Tibet and the
Tsinghai–Tibet roads had been constructed; and we Tibetans
had also participated,' the Tibetan workers tell me. The refer-
ence is of course to the serfs and runaways who, through road-
building, found out for the first time about wages, and more
important about their own human dignity. 'We had 86 motor
trucks and 120 workers in 1957, now we have 18 plants for
repair and maintenance of which this factory is one.' But it is
the oldest and the liaison centre for equipment distribution;
it is also the main centre for training new workers.

It was after the Cultural Revolution that expansion began; now there are 863 workers, 570 men, 293 women; 632 are Han workers, and 231 Tibetan workers, 154 men and 77 women. By 1974 the factory coped with repairs and maintenance for 712 trucks and lorries per year, established 4 workshops, with the possibility of coping with 112 repair points at a time, ensuring a swift turn-around. There is one assembly workshop, and one for turning out spare parts; the oxygen factory (organized in 1964, starting production in 1965) is also part of this road transport complex; oxygen tanks are available not only in Lhasa, but on the high passes, in case of 'sudden oxygen demand'.

In Tibet as elsewhere in China the Cultural Revolution was a turning point in accelerating industrialization. There is little documentation on what happened in Tibet during that time;[6] but the impetus derived from it is mentioned in the factories here. Previously, they say, the Liu Shao-chih 'capitalist roaders' considered Tibet a deficit area, expensive, and with no returns. Funds and technical expertise, and therefore industrialization, thus were not 'vigorously promoted' save in certain extractive and mining industries. But after the Cultural Revolution, 'Chairman Mao's line prevailed' and with it the notion of the autonomous region becoming a fully developed region, not a subsidiary of industries in other areas of China, and with it also, the rapid utilization of Tibetans themselves as workers in factories sited in Tibet.

The importance of this line, and its popularity, are obvious. 'Every young boy and girl now wants to become a worker, to drive a machine.' 'The Tibetans are very intelligent, they love machines and take great care of them,' say the Han cadres here. The national minorities all over China will themselves build up their own prosperity 'in the great motherland of China'; by developing their own workers, technicians, engineers, doctors, researchers, cadres, and 'contingents of theoreticians', innovators, intelligentsia. The workers are extremely conscious of this new role and responsibility. Tibet is not a 'colony' of

China, furnishing only raw materials; it can become a stupendous granary, and one of the wealthiest industrial regions in all Asia. And the first people to benefit by it must be the Tibetans themselves.

The introduction of Tibetan workers in factories accelerated after 1968, when the taboos on working in factories, which were strong, disappeared as a new generation of Tibetans came of age, propelled by the Cultural Revolution into accelerated progress.

I visit the workshops. Little has been spent on appearance; the innards, the machines, and especially the workers themselves are impressive. Haphazardly couched in the ample courtyards are trucks, and lorries; round them are Han and Tibetan workers. Apprentices, three to four to each group, Tibetans but also a few Hans, are learning about motors and what makes them work.

'In the beginning it was very slow. We did not understand machinery. We had no words for it. And we had fear, from the past.'

There are many 'old Tibetan workers' here; which means that they date from the early 1960s. In the workshops the banners are hung in both Han and Tibetan, with earnest slogans: 'Learn from Taching,'⁷ and 'Count on your own strength.' The machinery is neat and the Tibetan workers, mostly young, seem very able and conscientious. There is something very moving in the way they are wholly absorbed by the machines they work at.

I see how suddenly the old myths were exploded, the old world of belief crumbled, and a new logic, a new understanding of the world took its place. On the faces of these Tibetan workers, and in their speech, is all the excitement, the triumph of a new discovery, Science. 'We now know that it was not gods, not demons, that made the motors work. We handled them and we saw that it was not the blood of children that made them run, as the lamas told us.'

I shake hands with the foremen of the workshops; all

Tibetans, and among them a woman. Losangtumai, thirty-seven, has just returned from a university, he is now teaching technique in the night school for workers which functions within the factory. Ishitawa, thirty-five, has gone on a trip 'inland', to study trade unionism. He is the head of the new trade union here. There is a 'cultural centre', where workers read books and the newspapers, discuss events and politics, put on their own skits, dances and songs. Some of the Tibetan worker-cadres, I am told, are away, 'because the demand for Tibetan worker-cadres is very big, and they are till too few ... ' so they are travelling, to set up new factories. 'After all, we the workers are the leading class,' says Tandzemolo, thirty-five, who walks by my side.

The salaries for workers in Tibet are an average of 70 yuan per month, ranging from 63·83 to 140 yuan, higher than 'inland'. Apprentices get 36 yuan a month with food and lodging and work clothes and there is a 3-year apprenticeship. Since 1972, 200 apprentices, of whom 46 are from the high plateau, have come in.

The engineer is a Mr Sze, a worker engineer from Shanghai, thirteen years in Tibet; he is a buoyant, thin man, obviously popular with the Tibetan workers. He has not lost his Shanghai accent, but his complexion is now that of a Tibetan.

There are five canteens, in which all workers, whether Han or Tibetan, and the apprentices, eat together.[8] They live together, in exactly similar accommodation. 'Our Tibetan brothers make their own buttered tea,' but as far as food is concerned, they relish Han food and are taking to the more diversified diet with vegetables and rice. Here too sugar is added to the buttered tea.

From this factory, in 1968, a team of workers went to the Teachers' College, sited about two kilometres from Lhasa, and did what such teams of workers did in every Chinese university, a 'takeover'. Which means that they settled the problems which had been exposed during the Cultural Revolution, and also tried to orient education towards the concrete agricultural and industrial expansion.[9] A primary school for children is functioning within the precincts of the factory. Following the example of Taching, the factory owns some fields, situated twenty kilometres away, in which the families of the workers plant vegetables, breed cattle and pigs, thus 'feeding the factory'. The cadres among the workers (110 cadres out of 863 workers) work as the workers do, and also go in turn to labour in the fields, so that the distinction, worker or cadre, disappears. The large number of cadres is due to the fact that the 110 are also teachers, instructors, foremen and some are delegates to various levels of revolutionary committees.

We sit down after the visit for a leisurely talk. Mr Sze, the engineer, pours tea (not buttered) and tells me how tea is being grown in Tibet for 'self-sufficiency'. And how iodine is added to the salt in Tibet, where goitre is endemic.

I want some personal stories; how did the first Tibetan workers come here? What do they feel is their role, in New Tibet? The first to speak is curly-headed, handsome Tandzemolo ... After some prodding from his fellow-workers. 'I am from a blacksmith family. And the blacksmiths, in Tibet, were the most despised of all people bar the slaves. We were called "black bones", and other names.'

I later checked on this. I read in Huc[10] about the Pebouns, workers in metal, goldsmiths and jewellers; but Tandzemolo assured me that the blacksmiths were not included in that category. Class distinction was rigid in Old Tibet; and the only escape was to become a monk. The reason why blacksmiths were ill-considered was impiety; they manipulated iron and fire, and thus, by changing elements, defied the gods.

'My family was poor; at eight I was sent to become a lama in the monastery at Shigatze, to have a better life. But I was always being beaten; I carried water and wood and was despised as a "black bone". I was eighteen when the old order was overturned. The monastery doors were opened, many of us went out; we were sent to school or orphanages. I thought of becoming a blacksmith, but our brothers Han in the Army said:

"We need people like you," and I went to school for six months. Then I came here, in this repair factory, with other people who were blacksmiths, like me.'

Tandzemolo is a very good worker; very keen. When he first got to the factory, he wanted to know how everything worked. 'He spent his time unscrewing machines and then bolting them up again, just to find out how everything worked,' cried another worker, and everyone guffawed. Tandzemolo grinned. 'Go on, go on,' said someone to him. 'After 1964 I married ... I married a nun!'

I duly registered pleasurable surprise, and everyone was happy. Later I found out from the Hans in the revolutionary committee that 'some people even among Han cadres, objected to this marriage ... this was the old-fashioned, conservative thinking'. Which means that Tandzemolo had a 'struggle', both in his society, and even among some Han bureaucrats, to get social approval for his marriage. Tandzemolo earns 80 yuan a month, and so does his wife. They have two children at school. 'My mother had six children, now all have found work.' He became a Party member in 1973, and is going 'inland' for another six months to further his studies. He has also gone to a political school for six months, attends night school, and is obviously groomed to be a leading cadre; he is already a foreman, and member of the revolutionary committee of the factory.

Tandzemolo's wife, Lungochoka, was sent to the nunnery when she was 13. She says there were altogether round 12 to 13 thousand nuns in Tibet, one-tenth of the number of monks. Her mother had 8 children, 4 girls; 2 of the girls were sent to nunneries. 'There were about 80 nuns in the nunnery where I was, near Shigatze, 5 children about my age, a few others younger. Also some very old nuns, 60 or more. In 1957 my older sister who was a serf had been recruited by the PLA to go to Peking (to the Institute of National Minorities). She wrote me a letter, telling me that it was best to become a worker.[11] Then I went to seek work in a factory just opened in Shigatze.

Then I came to this factory. My little sister is in Lhasa Middle School, my elder sister is a bookkeeper in a county, one of my brothers is a worker at the hydro-electric plant near Lindze, another sister and another brother are workers in other parts of Tibet. We all live very well.'

Tentasuba, thirty-five, comes from Kongka. When he was three both his parents, agricultural serfs, died of hunger; he was sent by an aunt to the monastery; he was five. He became a domestic to a 'big lama', working, sweeping, cleaning floors, and 'I ran away when I was ten years old.'

Tentasuba then became a beggar. He slept in mounds of garbage and was very frightened of being bitten by dogs. 'I cried for father and mother but no one heard me. And there were many like me then in Tibet.' Then he became a slave cowherd for a noble when he was thirteen. 'I never had any shoes, and I wore only rags.' Then came the PLA. 'All the orphans were sent to schools. There were 160 of us orphan lamas. I was nineteen then, but I learnt to read and to write a little. Then in 1960 I came to this factory. I now have four children, and one of my children is going to be a PLA soldier. My wife is also a worker; we have a radio, two bicycles, and one watch, and we have saved 200 yuan, in the bank. The Han workers taught me all I know; and they had great patience. Now I have apprentices, learning from me. Our Tibetan old workers all have apprentices; and some of them are Han apprentices.'

This was correct. I saw, both in this factory and in another one, that among the apprentices were Hans, from the cities of China. In the winter of 1975, 300 more, from China's universities would be sent to serve apprenticeships in Tibet. The boost this gives to the emergent Tibetan working class can be imagined. It serves to do away with any superiority complex ('great Han chauvinism'). It also promotes mutual understanding between Han and the national minorities. All the apprentices live, eat, work together, and receive exactly the same salary, 36 yuan a month.

We have a great responsibility,' says Tentasuba. 'But it was only after the great proletarian Cultural Revolution that we understood this responsibility; that all levels of leadership must be in our hands, in the hands of the Tibetan proletariat. And we are the just born proletariat of the New Tibet.'

Tentasuba has been 'inland' twice, to Chengtu and Shanghai, to Wuhan, to Peking, to Hangchow. His wife was a beggar, from Chamdo. She and her mother begged their way from Chamdo to Lhasa, in the old days.

Fonka, a woman worker, thirty-seven years old, comes from Tsokon county in Chamdo territory. 'I became a servant at eight; my sister was a servant in the same nobleman's house because my mother had to repay a debt; I never saw my father. My mother was ill, she had tuberculous glands in the neck.[12] We prayed and prayed and gave butter and wool and meat to the lamas. But it was no use. Then because we had given away everything I became a beggar and carried my little brother on my back. In 1955 came the PLA and my mother's illness was cured by the PLA medical team stationed in the county; they came to our house, and looked after my mother, and gave us food. And so in 1956 I asked to go with them and they sent me to school. My mother washed clothes for the PLA, and helped them with the names of things and people, and showing them the mountain pathways. The first teacher in the school I went to was an interpreter with the PLA, who had come from Szechuan, her name is Chungtzo, and she put my name down to go to Peking to study. I was given a whole new set of clothes and I took the motorbus which the PLA had started, to go to Peking. It was the first time I had seen a motor bus. I studied almost eight years in the Institute of National Minorities in Peking, four years of culture and reading and writing, and three years of technique. I studied welding, and I am now a welder here. I graduated in 1963. My heart is full of happiness and I am still studying all the time. I teach welding, I have apprentices under me. My brother is at Nanking university, my husband is also a worker. We have two children.'

I visit the July 1 agricultural implements factory; here the revolutionary committee has four Tibetans and two Hans. Tudensijo is the vice-chairman; he was also a 'black bones', a blacksmith. 'We started this factory with a three-person team, all of us blacksmiths, making knives, cutters, scythes, in 1959. Soon we had formed a cooperative of 90 people, blacksmiths and ironmongers and also some carpenters. Then a small bicycle repair factory merged with us, and we were 120 in 1962. At first we turned out only ordinary agricultural implements; we did not know anything better. But in 1970 we began to make threshers. That was after the Cultural Revolution.

'We had never seen a thresher, nor any such machinery; two of our workers went to the inland and got a thresher. We also got planters for rice seedlings, and by that time we had electric power. We learnt about electric motors. And then our brother factories inland gave us the machine tools, ten of them. Come and see.'

So into the factory; the same sprawl of functional, barn-like workshops, but in them again the same air of neat efficiency. The cutters, grinders, and other machine tools are indeed there; with various labels: Shenyang, Tientsin, Shanghai, Peking ... they are old machines, but beautifully kept, and not one of them is idle. There are 40 women workers here; 160 of them altogether, all of them Tibetans.

This factory is now going to expand and become a tractor plant. Right now it is only assembling tractors, making some spare parts for those already in use; it also sends workers to repair machinery on the spot, in the rural areas. 'Only when this is not possible do we ask the villages to send the machinery into Lhasa.' There were 1,700 such 'visits' paid by the factory workers last year. Thus the educational role, and the integration of worker and peasant is brought about. All the factory foremen, the chairman and vice-chairman of the revolutionary committee are Tibetans. The two Hans are worker-engineers. Three Han worker-engineers from Manchuria have now come to help in the setting up of the tractor assembly and repair and the future tractor-making plant.

Tibetan workers have gone back and forth to the inland, to learn, to see machinery. 'All our work is based on self-reliance, self-study.' The Tibetan worker is a proud man, an intelligent man, and the factory exudes confidence. Here also are sixty-eight-year-old Solangtochieh and Kusawangtui, sixty; they were blacksmiths, and they insist on continuing to work, despite their age and pensions. They are also representatives on the revolutionary committee, and national delegates. 'Till I die I will work,' says Kusawangtui. As for Solangtochieh, he was so busy that he just nodded, never stopping work. He considers visitors a nuisance, obviously.

The factory is 'walking on two legs', which means that it continues making certain things by hand, such as planers and other simple tools and also handcarts (wheels for the village harvests). Here too are apprentices, 28 from each county in Tibet. 12 of the workers, 1 Han, 11 Tibetans, went to Sian last year to study more techniques. And 3 women workers are in universities in Chengtu, to learn technical expertise.

This factory for all its unsophisticated appearance, is a 'spawner', which means that it is already providing workers to a web of other factories, at lower level, which are constituted with little capital investment, and whose spread provides at low transport cost, services over a wide area.

Of the 252 factories in Tibet, there are 29 in Lhasa municipality. The cement factory on the road to Tsinghai is new and chiefly manned by Hans. Being out of town, it is probably more difficult to get Tibetan manpower here; the countryside can hardly spare many. 'Everywhere it is the same problem. There is a great need for Tibetan workers, for Tibetan cadres, for agricultural cadres; with a grounding in mechanization of agriculture as well as in improved agronomic techniques.' Meanwhile already the Shanghai workers of Lindze wool textile factory are less than 50 per cent of the total, gradually replaced by Tibetans. The electric battery factory has 200

Tibetans and Hans, who together first constructed the factory, before it went into production.

The Tibetan rug and carpet factory of Lhasa is also deceptively small from the outside, some buildings of Tibetan style, but the windows are large and the rooms luminous and airy. There, on primitive looms, carpets are hand made, but the wool has been prepared in Lindze, and dyed there. All the 115 workers are Tibetan, 40 men and 75 women, some are very young, round 18.

The director is comrade Yu, a small, neat woman from Manchuria who came to Tibet in 1955. She and two Tibetan men run the factory.

The biggest rug factory is in Gyantze, although this one in Lhasa is already a State factory, organized in 1953 from the carpet-makers who worked for the nobility. Old workers from the famous Tientsin and Peking rug factories came here, on the demand of the local Tibetan government, who did not mind more carpets being made, so long as there was no 'mechanization'. One of these Han experts stayed here, and married a Tibetan girl. In 1972 export of Tibetan rugs began again, but 'we also have to cater for the demand of the internal market'. The demand in rugs, wall carpets, and covers for beds is growing, especially in pastoral areas. Fewer and fewer men and women spin their own wool, weave their own aprons, and the thick coarse wool for robes which literally never left their owner's body is no longer liked; the habits, and also the clothing, of the younger generation are changing.

I notice that the patterns of the carpets made are quite varied. Some are Tibetan, but there are others which adapt the Tientsin 'cut-out' style. 'Yes, we adopted techniques from Tientsin and Peking carpets, but sometimes it did not turn out too well,' says comrade Yu, cheerfully. 'For instance the dragon. We made some Tibetans rugs with dragons on them, but we gave them the usual Chinese five claws; purchasers complained they were not genuine Tibetan; the old Tibetan dragons had only four claws ... '

Wall carpets are now being made, showing scenes of Lhasa, complete with Potala above, broad avenue with motorbus below. Minawangtui, thirty-eight years old, a veteran Tibetan worker, and Chiangpapantsin, thirty-five, both when children carpet-makers at Gyantze, both in the factory's revolutionary committee now, are helping to resurrect some of the 170-odd traditional designs of Tibetan carpets, 'we have an expansion plan,' they tell me. 'First, more internal production, to cater for our own people and their growing demand. Second, to continue to expand our export production at the Canton fair. Thirdly, to increase the mechanization of the process. Fourthly, we aim to have our own dye factory, to deal with the primary product.' Many carpet cooperatives are already joining forces in order to achieve this expansion.

The factory also runs a nursery for children; over 20 of them are here. The salary is more than 60 yuan, which is around 3 to 5 yuan more than the average carpet factories I visited in Tientsin and Peking some years ago. The factory also has vegetable plots, keeps pigs, and runs a canteen. Many of the girls are pretty and light complexioned, they are probably city girls.

In Lhasa's emporium and other shops industrial goods from light industries in Tibet, as well as those that are still brought from China, are on sale. But the stamp 'Made in Tibet' is on the matchboxes, which once were imported; on the boots and shoes, which are found in large quantities, and very well made, on flashlight batteries, on many of the wool clothes, felts, knitted garments and on the balls of wool thread sold here. It is also possible, through the emporium, to order a pair of shoes, and have them made to measure in the leather cooperatives. Here all wool and wool cloth is in bright colours, the rainbow colours Tibetans love. There are vases, and glasses from the glass factory; cheek by jowl with wooden tsampa bowls, Thermos flasks, and pressure cookers; plastics are also here, basins, and pails and aprons. There are drinking mugs made in Sian and Chengtu. Nylon is also here. The handwoven wool aprons still worn by Tibetan girls were heavy and unwashable. More and more one sees the young in the cities wearing easily washable nylon aprons, striped to look like the genuine old apron. There are also many blouses, of cotton, of nylon, of satiny stuff, printed, flowered, checked, pink, blue, green. There are cotton shirts and drip-dry shirts for men, and padded jackets, trousers, Chinese style. There is tinned meat, flour, sugar and milk in tins. There is no yak butter; almost every home can get its own. There are Szechuan pickles (for the Han cadres, many of whom are Szechuanese). There are electric batteries, flashlights, pots and pans, agricultural instruments, spades and hoes and rakes. There are bicycles and sewing machines and radios and also a few watches. Behind the counters are Tibetan girls and Han girls, in almost equal number. The crowd of shoppers is varied. There are Hans since Lhasa city has probably a higher proportion of Hans, being the administrative centre, and also a military garrison as well as an industrial and transport centre. But many Tibetans are here too, so that the place looks a little like the courtyard of the Menzekang, a motley of garbs and headgear. The smell of yak butter is strong.

I hear—it is only a rumour—that to speed up agricultural mechanization and industrialization railways are a-building and also a pipeline to carry petrol from the refineries of Kansu and Szechuan to Tibet. The railway from Chengtu to Kumming, completed four years ago, will be joined by another railway, crossing the mountains and the major rivers, from Chengtu to Lhasa. This is a formidable undertaking, but then, a visit to Lhasa convinces one that nothing is impossible. The pipeline is important, for 30 per cent of the lorries must carry the oil for the journey.[13]

These are the new miracles, exorcizing the abject terrors of the past. Perhaps, to some Tibetans, the machine is still 'a new god'. And certainly, there must be among the 200 upper-class families that remain, some who regret the past. There must still be a good many who still believe in reincarnation and in demons that ambush the soul. But Tandzemolo, speaking of the solar converters—another project which is being realized, says:'We can now harness the sun and the waters and the wind. We are no longer afraid.' And he, and others like him, the working class of Tibet, know the future is theirs.

7

A Kingdom of Women

Since woman's liberation is an essential component of the Chinese Revolution, I interviewed members of the federation of women in Tibet, and also met as many women cadres as possible, to ascertain how this question was dealt with in the region.

A difficulty cropped up. All these cadres were young, the oldest being forty, the youngest twenty-eight. They spoke a great deal about woman in New Tibet, but were reluctant to speak of the old society except in opprobrious terms. I could understand their rejection of all it had meant, in terror and suffering, and why they emphasized their new role and power. But I needed some background on social conditions and how they affected women before 1959.

It is curious how little former travellers paid attention to the condition of woman in Tibet, how little they wrote about her. The British who wrote a good deal on Lhasa's 'mysteries' seem almost too reticent on the subject, except to point out that polyandry existed.

Early Chinese travellers spoke of the geographical area which is Tibet today as the Kingdom of Women. It was marked thus in maps of the eighth century.[1] In the *Western Pilgrimage*, that splendid Chinese story translated by Arthur Waley as *The Monkey*, there is mention of adventures in a kingdom where women reign, and men are subordinate to them. Songtsang Kampo, first King of Tibet, is said to have greatly admired and honoured women, and legends and tales of such a country 'in the West' persisted in Chinese literature for a good many centuries, but were no longer identified with Tibet. For lamaism destroyed the matriarchal society which probably existed here. Not only lamaism, but among the nobility the influence of Chinese Confucianism (though unrecognizable as such) led to a lowered status for woman. As a result Tibetan mores, where women are concerned, are complex and vary from class to class and area to area.

Our invaluable observer, Père Huc, tells us that 'immorality' had known no bounds in Tibet until a great Lama ordered that women, when going out, should rub on their faces a black, glutinous varnish (reported to be made of sheep's blood with yak butter) to make themselves ugly looking. This apparently had some effect in reducing temptation for the lamas, but 'the Tibetans are far from being exemplary in the matter of morality ... lamentable licentiousness'. He noted 'the women there enjoy very great liberty. Instead of vegetating, prisoners in the depths of their houses, they lead an active and laborious life ... In the rural districts, it is the women who perform most of the labours of agriculture ... The men ... less laborious and active ... occupy themselves especially with spinning and weaving wool ... '

All sins (and carnality was a sin, since celibacy was holiness) were ascribed to the woman. Hence the idea of pollution, associated with woman, with childbirth. No woman was allowed to touch a lama's belongings, nor could she raise a wall, or 'the wall will fall'. She was not allowed to dig canals, or 'the water will not go through'.[2] The widow was a despicable being, already a devil. No woman was allowed to use iron instruments or touch iron. Religion forbade her to lift her eyes above the knee of a man, as serfs and slaves were not allowed to lift the eyes upon the face of the nobles or great lamas. If she gave birth to twins she was liable to death by burning as a witch.

The laws, or customs (the word law does not fit in a land where all depended on religious *diktat* and the whims of the lords, and officials) about rape are worth noticing. Should a woman be raped 'against her will', she had to pay one silver coin; and if 'consenting to rape' she paid three silver coins.

In a serf and slave society there is no such thing as 'marriage' in the sense that western society knows it, and no official registration of such unions. Each class had its own marriage and sexual customs, and what the aristocracy could do was not allowed to the rest of the population.

In the aristocracy, woman enjoyed a great deal of freedom as compared to Chinese society and even to western society until recent times. She could go out freely; she rode on horseback; (serfs were not allowed to ride). She could, and did, own property. But marriage was arranged by the parents, and polygamy was frequent. An auspicious day was chosen, after consultations with the lamas and when all property arrangements were considered satisfactory. The bride went on a horse, and wrapped to the eyes, to the groom's home, weeping copiously all the way in sign of filial piety.[3]

The husband was permitted any number of concubines; and divorce appears to have been easy if both sides wanted it and divided up the property, with the man taking the boys and the woman the girl children.

But this marriage custom involved only a ridiculously small percentage, the 200 families of the upper class. Polygyny was also practised among them; one man marrying several sisters in a family.

What happened among the multitude of serfs, slaves and herdsmen? Although Winnington says that 'Tibetan woman regards polyandrous marriage as an institution conferring great prestige on woman',[4] I don't believe him. He got this information from a man, to begin with; and secondly, I just don't see how any prestige or self-respect can redound to the credit of a woman compelled to marry up to five men, not of her choosing, because they are brothers. She becomes the 'labouring beast' for all of them. This custom of polyandrous marriage was dictated by compelling economic conditions and nothing else. It predominated among the serfs, herdsmen on the plateaux, was found much less in the cities, nor did it occur among the slaves (200,000 of them).

The woman did all the heavy work except pasturing the herds: milking, churning the butter, preparing the tsampa, and having the children. And sex with two, three, four men must have been added labour.

The scanty property of herdsmen—a cow, some sheep, a yak—while they grazed the vast herds belonging to monasteries and noble houses, also meant that a herdsman was allowed a small piece of land as his own. In order not to subdivide this land the several sons of a family would marry one wife. A wife belonged technically to the eldest son, who shared her with his brothers; if they married separately, they lost all rights in the wife and in any of the children that resulted, for all children belonged to the eldest son.

And this custom was not dictated by scarcity of women; since polygyny also existed, and for the same compelling reason, to prevent subdividion of herd or land. Thus a family with many daughters would 'buy' a husband for them all.

Among the serfs, there was no protection for marriage or the family. To begin with no ceremony was conducted, as a result the man could abandon his wife and family who were without redress. Poverty separated many couples, the woman going begging, the man either trying to peddle or to carry firewood. Serfs were not allowed to marry without their owners' consent. Since marriage often removed an able-bodied man from a village—for the custom was for the man to join the woman's village, and not the other way round, because woman was the more valuable labour power of the two—the serf-owner would only consent when a replacement—another serf—could be exchanged, if the woman was some-one else's serf. The sentence 'I never knew my father' which I heard from two of the women I interviewed, does not indicate a philandering male; serfs were sold at will; and could be sepa-rated at will. A number of Tibetan cadres only mentioned their mothers in their talks to me.

As for slaves, and 'black bones' like the blacksmiths, the situation was even worse. Slaves could be raped or used at will by their masters. Marriage did not exist for them. 'Nobody married a blacksmith' was what the workers of blacksmith origin had told me.

The idea that lamas were celibate, holy men, also does not stand close examination. Not only was homosexuality rampant (with the hundreds of young boys crowding into each monastery to become lamas) but lamas roaming in the countryside could have women at will; and no one dared to deny them. Brothels seem to have been fairly common; though of course officially deplored, both in Lhasa and other towns.

The members of the woman's federation of Tibet I interviewed were all from serf, slave or servant background. It is not surprising that they gave me the dimmer aspects of a woman's life and not the view of a gay noblewoman clad in furs and silks, sauntering on horseback, with a headdress of pearls and turquoise. Their stories were similar to those I might have had interviewing a family of Blacks in America just out of slavery. Family life does not exist when men and women and their offspring are objects, at the disposal of their owner.

To raise the Tibetan woman's consciousness of her new role in a new society, was on the one hand very difficult due to the religious terror, and superstition ... On the other, it seems to me it was in some ways easier than in Confucian China. Oppression of women in Tibet was linked to religion, yet at the same time no lay person, and woman least of all, was admitted to participate in the religious cult. True, she attended occasional festivals celebrated by the monasteries; and the intercessions, by prayers and exorcisms, of the lamas in case of sickness. But she was all the time an outcast. Perhaps that is why, whereas one-fifth of the male population was celibate, only one-fifteenth of the female population was in nunneries. This discrepancy was also due to woman's essential role as the heavy labourer, both in pastoral and in agricultural areas, and therefore the real provider, A family could do without the male; it could not do without the woman, the mother, and to be exempt from *corvée*, a woman had to pay more than a man.

Hence the paradox: the Tibetan woman appears to me more 'revolutionary', ready to revolt, because her exploitation has been so great. Since she was kept out of religious ritual though not free from religious extortion, once she realized that her labour was a strength, her repudiation of that system was all the more forceful. Photographs of serfs at mass meetings, demanding land reform, denouncing exploitation, show a large proportion of women actively taking part. Whereas in north China, for instance, until round 1959 there were still women confined at home, who replied when work teams knocked on the door: 'No one is at home,' because they had no right to speak to anyone except their own close family. Here in Tibet because women were the workers, out in the fields, because they travelled as carriers, as pedlars, they did not suffer, when speaking at mass meetings, the accusation of 'going against nature'. And foot binding never occurred in Tibet.

'All men and women are equal,' was the slogan of the first women's organizations.

In 1959, when religion as a ruling system was destroyed, women were already going to the antenatal clinics at the hospital in Lhasa, and coming to the hospital for confinement; the awareness of 'a different life' was more persuasive than any speaking. 'Our children do not die any more.' Then came the communes, and the workpoints, and from the very start women earned a good deal, even more than men.

Pengto, twenty-nine years old, from the county of Kangma, is from a family of slave herders. 'We had no clothes or shoes. There were many wolves, and when they killed the sheep we were responsible. I kept sheep when I was seven years old.' Her father spun and wove to make pulu cloth for their master. He was beaten and had one eye gouged out because he fell asleep and the cloth was spoilt. When she was thirteen the PLA came, and Pengto was recruited, and organized a children's association. They learnt songs and dances, and later she participated in land reform, 'struggle' meetings (against the former serf-owners). She then went to the Institute of National Minorities from 1960 to 1964; she was nineteen years old when she graduated. In 1965 she participated in the establishment of the communes. 'Since we, the women, did the labour, of course, the communes were good for us.'

She and other young women like her, became Tibetan Red Guards at the Cultural Revolution. And the Cultural Revolution, for the women in Tibet, was a turning point. The 'four olds', old traditions, customs, behaviour, ways of thinking, were all violently denounced. Polygamy, polygyny and polyandry stopped.

Since polyandry was guided by economic reasons, once the pastoral herdsmen were in communes, with security and a raised standard of living the need for polyandry disappeared. Polygamy practised by the upper classes is of course extinct since this class no longer exists. The lamas who came out of monasteries were eager to get married, and marriages of lamas also tore the fabric of belief to shreds. Polygyny also went, since many lamas were from the pastoral plateaux, and became available as husbands.

Ishichoma, forty years old, came from the Khampa district, where she said, 'there were two monks for one layman'. This plethora of monks in the Kantze (Khampa) district she could not explain. The monasteries were exceptionally powerful there. The 'warlike' Khampas, held up for so long as estimable heroes for their participation in the rebellion of 1959, were for a large part embattled lamas. Although the district of Kantze was not under Lhasa's direct administration, nor had been, since the end of the Ming dynasty, 'everything was like in Tibet'. It was the abolition of 'ula' which provoked the monasteries into revolt. 'Now in Kantze Tibetan autonomous district there is only monogamous marriage.'

In Tibet there are slightly more women than men (51·4 per

cent of women versus 48·6 per cent of men), so 'women's organizations here are very important, and woman remains an important labour force. That is why in these sixteen years the Tibetan woman has entered every leadership level.'

'The change of attitude is really very striking,' says Ishichoma. She cites examples of women taking leading roles in promoting changes and progress. I have already mentioned a few, such as the midwife Pasang Tzuchen, such as Pasang, such as Tsomo. There are many others. In one county, all the posts of secretary or vice-secretary of revolutionary committees are held by women; in another, 32 out of 71 cadres are women. Ishichoma herself is now going to direct the commercial department in Lhasa, becoming vice-department head. Out of around 27,000 Tibetan cadres, 12,000 are women cadres. And out of the 6,400 barefoot doctors, a little over half are women.

Women of the upper class also joined the women's federation in the early 1950s. Before 1959, some of them were also active, 'but there is always class struggle because they did not really want to lose their privilege. Of course, we have some who actively cooperate with us even today, when our work is mainly directed towards the base.' The wife of the nobleman Ngapo Nawang Jigme is still one of the leaders of the women's federation. But the sheer number and weight of serf-women, ex-slaves, makes the participation of noblewomen more a figurehead than a really active force, since there were so few. However, Ngapo Nawang Jigme and his wife are always spoken of with immense respect and affection; she is also a very well-known singer, and has given many concerts all over China.

In the revolutionary museum in Lhasa, an exhibition of clay figures made by artists here shows 'the revolt of the serfs'. Women figure prominently in it especially one called Hola-mutsung, she seems to have led a serf revolt some time in the 1920s. For this she appears, like Joan of Arc, to have been burnt alive.

The women I interview talk of their own lives, how they

were changed; the problem of having children, and also developing their own personalities. 'For this it is necessary to have nurseries, to have all the help possible.' For these women cadres, family planning is already individually acceptable and practised; I notice that most of them have no more than four children.

In old Tibet, society was divided into three classes, with three degrees in each class. The top nobles and top lamas, who were also the top officials, and the 'others', that is serfs, slaves and house domestics. Punishments varied according to class. If a high prelate or noble killed a serf, he was automatically absolved, a second degree noble paid 10 copper coins, a third degree noble or religious paid 20 copper coins. If it was proved that the killing was 'without reason' then the magistrate (noble or official) would do something (usually a small fine) but no one dared to take the risk of proving a case, because, if the reason was found insufficiently grave, the family who complained would be punished for 'insolence', and sold into slavery. And 'insolence' itself was sufficient 'reason' to kill a serf ...

With all this behind them, can one be surprised at the enthusiasm with which the Tibetan woman is responding to the change that has taken place in her life? 'The Tibetan woman is an extraordinary driving force,' says Comrade Chen, who admires them greatly. 'They are not bashful, self conscious and they are very energetic.' 'Also the dancing. Our Tibetan sisters dance so much better than we do. And how they sing!'

A Tibetan woman, Panthog, climbed Mount Everest in 1975. Tibetan women doctors, workers, engineers, dancers, singers, sportswomen are coming out of this new generation of women. Tibet may not be a Kingdom of Women, but the women of Tibet are certainly among the most gifted and capable I have met.

8

Education and Autonomy

Almost every country in the world today is a mosaic of several ethnic groups; and one of the features of the present world is the demand for the revival of language and culture, an ethnic identity, which sometimes expresses itself violently. Witness the troubles generated in France, where Basque, Breton, and Corsican now claim either autonomy or since autonomy is not satisfactorily granted to them, go on to want total separation from the mother country.

In the continent that is China, fifty-five formally identified nationalities exist. People who reproach China with having 'destroyed' these ethnic groups, would do well to consider how little, in Europe, and even in England, such minority claims have received respect or regard. Indeed, had some of these countries done as much as China has done in the last twenty-five years in that regard, perhaps there would be less turbulence and violence in certain western nations.

After the installation of the People's Republic of China and the new Central Government in 1949, the latter immediately defined the right to autonomy in its Constitution (promulgated 1954).[1] I have, in the last twenty years, paid special attention to the topic of national minorities, and travelled extensively in minority areas, meeting altogether round nineteen minorities and can testify that the policy of autonomy is being scrupulously carried out, especially since the Cultural Revolution brought out many able, young people in these areas and promoted them to leadership posts.

Had the Han Chinese tried to impose—as America has done

—one language, one culture, one set of habits, customs upon its diverse ethnic groups the turbulence which is now on the increase in western Europe (where minority languages do not have equal status) would also trouble the Peope's Republic of China.

China's fifty-four minorities range from the Was of Yunnan Province, several hundred in number, who are at the Stone Age, whose vocabulary consists only of around 600 words, and who do not count numbers beyond two; to the very sophisticated cultures of the Islamic Uighurs in Sinkiang who utilized Arabic script until very recently.[2] The People's Republic even went so far as to create a new written language for several minorities who had none; they established schools in those languages where there had never been any.

Today 40 per cent of China's territory is enjoying autonomy rights, since the 8 per cent of the population which comprise the fifty-four minorities do occupy this extent of territory. The minorities do not practise family planning, unless they wish it—it is a right under the autonomy concept of the nationality itself.

In Tibet, preparation for autonomy began with the preparatory committee instituted in 1956, with the Dalai Lama and Panchen Lama at their head. Because of the turbulence from serf-owners and the lamas, major reforms were postponed till 1962, and 90 per cent of all the Chinese technical personnel which—with the Dalai Lama's assent—had come into Tibet to help set up clinics, hydro-electric plants, to institute a system of loans to the indebted rural areas, were withdrawn.

It is strange to note that, after this forbearance, the Dalai Lama, in one of his contradictory statements—accused the Hans of 'hindering reforms' that he was planning to carry out. It was only after his departure that reforms, led by the Tibetans themselves, could begin. But the first few years were, of course, difficult; one difficulty pointed up in interviews was 'the Liu Shao-chi' line.

The Liu Shao-chi line also called 'capitalist roader or revi-sionist'[3] was fundamentally detrimental to the minorities, because it denied funds to deficit areas, and cut down on tech-nical aid, education, and development, concentrating resources on profit-making areas. Tibet has been, until 1974, a massively deficitary area in all sectors.[4] With Mao Tsetung's 'proletarian line' coming into prominence, funding has doubled in the last ten years (increased twelve times in certain sectors, such as education for the promotion of Tibetan cadres, and in the health sector). With the present agricultural mechanization programme, we may expect investments in this sector also to increase notably as well as industrial development oriented towards agricultural mechanization and electrification.

The Cultural Revolution in Tibet is not well documented. Already in September 1966, it is said, there were Red Guards forming in the teachers' college of Lhasa, and also in Lhasa's secondary school, the two institutes of higher education in Tibet at the time. Factional clashes occurred in Tibet as else-where and it would have been surprising if at the time attempts by erstwhile serf-owners and lamas to incite local troubles had not occurred. On September 18, 1967, a 5-point directive for-bidding armed clashes in Tibet was passed by the Central leaders in Peking; and a 'preparatory' group for a great alliance was formed. But it was another year before clashes ceased. The restoration of order, together with a 'correct orientation' is credited to Jen Yung, Political Commissar in Tibet. 'It was a very complicated class struggle,' is the usual formula that one gets. 'However, we persisted in Chairman Mao's line.' The Tibet revolutionary committee was set up on September 8, 1968, and Tseng Yung-ya, acting commander of the PLA in Tibet, and Jen Yung were named its chairman and vice-chair-man. Ngapo Nawang Jigme, the aristocrat, once minister to the Dalai Lama, remained vice-chairman of the revolutionary committee (as well as vice-chairman of the standing committee of the National People's Congress). Recently Tseng Yung-ya was named to another post and Jen Yung became acting chairman while Tien Pao, a Tibetan from Apa[5] became the second vice-chairman and second political commissar. Both Jen Yung and Tien Pao are Long Marchers, and I had the great honour and pleasure to meet both of them.

Far from repressing 'national aspirations' therefore, Tibet is quite exemplary in its promotion, through the people mentioned above, of active, young, and vigorous Tibetan cadres at all levels. The emphasis placed on autonomy as a truly democratic process of ethnic representation, within the larger unity of China, has been very perceptible in the last five years. It is for the Tibetan people eminently satisfactory and extremely popular. Out of 8 top-level leaders, 4 are Tibetans, of whom 2 are women; and of these 4 Tibetans 2 are in their early thirties.

I had occasion to speak with Tien Pao informally. Tien Pao was a boy of fifteen or so when, in 1935, the soldiers of the Red Army, led by Mao Tsetung, traversed Szechuan on the Long March, and passed through his district, Apa. Tien Pao belonged to a poor family, and he had seen his parents make a pilgrimage to Lhasa to obtain a 'better life'. He joined the Red Army when it marched through Apa in the summer of 1935, and he and other young Tibetans he recruited acted as guides through the great marshes which the Red Army traversed.[6]

In Yenan, Mao Tsetung organized detachments of national minorities, and Tien Pao became a Party member in 1937 and led the Tibetan contingent. It is from that time that his name, Tien Pao, was given to him by Mao Tsetung. It means: 'Heaven's gift'. Mao, a sensitive man, never forgot the hideous poverty of the national minorities nor the way they were oppressed, not only by their overlords, but also by greedy Han officials and merchants who rifled, pillaged, and ill-used them. As soon as liberation came in 1949, his first concern was for the national minorities. They must have everything, and perhaps even more, than what was being done for the Han people. The first medical teams were sent to the national minorities; and Mao's policies consistently laid emphasis on a special effort to pour government funds into national minority areas, in order to help them attain the same overall standard as the rest of China and not remain lagging behind as 'secondary regions'. The Institutes of National Minorities in many cities saw the best of China's brains come to teach the national minorities. And far from apprehending the development of 'separatist' tendencies, the Central Government under Mao's leadership contend that only when 'large contingents' of the national minorities are trained as cadres for their own people, as theoreticians, experts, and the areas become self-sufficient will China have truly accomplished a socialist brotherhood.

The policy therefore is not to overwhelm, overrun, and 'sinicize' the minorities, but precisely the opposite. With this in view marriage between Han and national minorities was forbidden *to the Hans*, the reason being that in the past, too many Han officials and rich men had abducted, as concubines, the girls of the national minorities. Later, however, marriage between Han women and national minority men was allowed; reversing the process whereby a 'superior' people discriminate against the males of a minority, while integrating the women, and thus provoking resentment. At the moment, there is no bar at all in marriages between minorities and the majority Han; for the stage of equality has been reached. If marriage is still rare (although cases of Han cadres marrying Tibetan women, and then remaining all their lives in Tibet, were cited to me) that is natural; intermarriage has always been the exception rather than the custom. However, intermarriage is well looked upon now. The niece of a friend of mine, the daughter of a well-known physician of Shanghai, married a Kazakh herdsman when she became a barefoot doctor in Sinkiang,[7] and is now living in tents, in a Kazakh pastoral commune, totally integrated with her husband's ethnic group. Her story was printed as praiseworthy in the national newspaper, the *People's Daily*.

'The policy in Tibet, as in every national minority, is to

promote vigorously a large number of Tibetan cadres at *all* levels,' said Tien Pao to me; not to have Han administration imposed upon and lording it over Tibetan people.

Today, below county level (seventy-three counties in Tibet) all cadres are of Tibetan nationality, at the district, commune and team levels, in all sectors of activity. At county level, 60 per cent of the cadres are of Tibetan nationality, and, as we have seen, 50 per cent at the top level.

In the factories (252 in 1975) replacement of Han workers by Tibetan workers goes on. The working class is *the* cradle for leadership cadres of the future, as well as for the new intelligentsia and the political theoreticians. Thus in the factories of Lindze already 50 to 60 per cent of the workers are Tibetans.

In the State farms run by the PLA, the majority of workers – which also means trainees in agronomics, and in techniques such as driving tractors, maintenance of equipment – are Tibetans.

This leads us to the problem of education. Since education was still in the throes of a grand debate in China as recently as April 1976, it was interesting to find out how Tibet handled this problem.

The 4,300-odd primary schools established since 1959 teach in Tibetan until the age of 14 or 15, and 27 of them continue in Tibetan, for a first year of lower middle school. Owing to the enhanced standard of living, some of these schools in rural areas are now entirely supported by the communes which they serve, and the problem since 1974 is no longer funding, but remains the great dearth of teachers. To fill this gap, the Lhasa Teachers' College, and the Lhasa Higher Middle School are speeding up their own expansion.

These are the two establishments of higher education in Lhasa and there are plans to form an additional scientific and research institute. But at the present moment, the main problem encountered, when education reaches the middle school level, is language.

I spent an afternoon at the Lhasa Secondary School,

established on the site where Lhasa's first primary school was started in 1955. Winnington, who visited it then, expressed himself delighted to see the sons of nobles and their private child-servants, sons of serfs, sitting together. But 'appearances are deceptive' said the present director of the school, Mr Wei.[8] Although noble and servant did attend the school together, the servant remained a servant. He carried his master's books, and even if he received tuition, he could never be more than a servant. In the Institutes for National Minorities there had been some trouble between 1956 and 1959 because Tibetan aristocratic youths refused to make their beds, clean their rooms or mingle with the orphans and escaped slaves. Interference by the lamas at the primary school occurred daily. Each day prayers before and after the study sessions had to be performed (as Winnington also reported). Lamas were sent to 'oversee' education and were on the school committee. Only in 1959 did all this disappear.

It is quite clear that, although a minimum of devotion is still allowed among the people, lamas are no longer permitted to teach religion in any way. And since previously the only 'teaching' was by lamas as private teachers to the nobility or in monasteries, there is no way for lamaism to survive in Tibet.

After 1959 the students of the Lhasa Primary School were required to do what was being done all over China: to engage in 'productive labour', cultivate vegetable plots, wash their own clothes, and help in the harvesting round Lhasa, since it was in those years (1958–60) that the reform of education, and integration by labour for all the young was part of education, was started.

But, said the director, between 1961 and 1965 education fell 'in the hands of the revisionists' under Liu Shao-chi. The school remained 'a closed organization'.[9] Labour by the students— promoting integration with the peasants—was abandoned. 'There was no reality to the teaching, it was abstract.' And no real effort was made to build up Tibetan cadres, a new intelligentsia out of the liberated serfs, to promote self-reliance for the region through the small and medium factories which Mao Tsetung had promoted in China. In 1960 the primary school added a secondary and an upper secondary level; the first 500 graduates came out in 1964.

Then came the Cultural Revolution. Criticism of 'revisionist' education started, and 'at last Chairman Mao's policies, integration of the youth with workers and peasants' were put into practice. The school began to change. It oriented the curriculum towards practice, towards 'workers and peasants', bringing up worthy and dedicated young people who did not despise manual labour. Until then, according to the director, the teaching had merely promoted contempt for work.

I went round the campus and its brick buildings, with physics and chemistry laboratories, and a library, as well as classrooms. I noticed that many of the glass windows were broken; this is a relic of the juvenile clashes which took place during the Cultural Revolution, and since glass windows are not a priority and still have to be imported, it may be some time before they are replaced. But this does not depress either the director or his staff. 'We have a lot of fresh air,' they said, laughingly.

There are now 23 classes, and 1,133 students, and out of these 582 are Tibetan, the others are Hans. This large concentration of Han youths surprised me; until I found out that they were the children of practically all the Han cadres in Tibet; and since Lhasa is an administrative centre, many Hans are here in Lhasa.

This brought me to the question: how many Hans are there in Tibet? From what I could ascertain definitely, by asking different people, between 250,000 to 300,000, counting also the army garrisons and the large State farms, and also the maintenance teams on the roads, as well as the teaching, medical, and industrial personnel. Reports that 'millions of Hans' had 'invaded Tibet' are not only fancy, they are absurdities, showing a total ignorance of the conditions here. It is absolutely impossible to transport 'millions' to Tibet, and had they walked the several thousand miles, they would have starved on the way, since it would have taken, on the average, three months on foot, across fourteen mountain passes, and without any food available on the way.

And there is also altitude sickness; the fact that the Hans who come here must submit to a rigorous medical examination before coming.

Only 176 Han university graduates have 'settled permanently' in Tibet since 1972; and only 300 are scheduled to come in the winter of 1975.

Thus, apart from the army, which has to assure the defence of the very long frontier and the road maintenance, I would estimate that only 50,000 personnel in all sections are Han, and even they return every two years for a three-month spell with their families. Few of the families come here; but it does happen, especially in the case of women cadres sent to Tibet, that they have to take their children with them.

While at the Secondary School, then, the proportion of Hans is large, there are none at the Teacher's Institute, where all the students are Tibetan. They are 1,200 at present; 1,280 are in training in Institutes for National Minorities in Chengtu, Peking, Kunming; and 720 in medical schools outside Tibet. 1,300 more will be sent this year (1976).

And this is where the problem of language becomes important. For the Tibetan language, until now, was not adequate for teaching science, superior mathematics, biology, or medicine. Although it can cope with simple arithmetic, it cannot cope with chemistry or physics, without mentioning such things as biochemistry, physiology, or higher levels of scientific training.

This problem is common to a good many countries of the Third World, whose languages have to be expanded, transformed, to include many new words, in order to become efficient vehicles for twentieth-century science. The Chinese language began this mighty effort in the early twentieth century, at the time of the first Cultural Revolution of 1919. It is now able to create terms for any developing science, including astrophysics, cybernetics, and molecular biology.

But Tibetan was profoundly and solely a religious, liturgical language. Until 1959 it did not have words for atom, dynamo, aeroplane, lorry; and its considerable religious vocabulary was also unknown to most of the Tibetans themselves, since it was highly abstruse metaphysics.

Although fabulously wealthy in names of gods and their various avatars, the Tibetan language is extremely poor in abstract or generic terms, or categorization of concrete objects. Thus there is a name for every kind of tree (willow, poplar, etc.) but no general word 'tree'. There is no word for 'cavalry' or 'harness' although the bridle of a horse is separated into thirty different parts, each one with its own name. There are also dozens of terms to designate the different depths of meditation, or trance, but no general word for 'sleep'.

Tibetan had thus become two languages: one used by the monks, written on parchment, endless repetitive religious formulae, and the other, the spoken language of the people, a colloquial vehicle considered 'base'. Even this spoken language varied from place to place. There was also a 'court language', spoken by the nobles and the high prelates between themselves, with complicated formulae denoting rank, hierarchy, and respect for superiors.

Although in 1956 a twelve-man committee was set up to tackle the language problem and to start a Han-Tibetan dictionary, progress was slow, since the committee was chiefly composed of nobles. New words did not spread among the people. The same difficult was encountered in India when Hindi was declared the national language. New terms had to be invented for common objects, such as 'tennis racket', but they proved very unwieldy, until the people themselves devised such words.

The staff at the Secondary School discussed this problem with me. Of the 74 teachers, 31 Tibetan, 43 Han, 10 were hard at work on a revised Han-Tibetan dictionary. During the past

16 years 100,000 new terms and words have come into Tibetan, and the 'court' language has been abandoned. Except for the remaining lamas, the religious language is no longer used.

But the written language was entirely religious. As a result, it had not varied from the old spelling, while the common, or usual words, had changed. For instance, the word for rice, pronounced *de*, was written *hbras*, and the word *U* (the Dalai Lama's territory) pronounced *Woo*, was written *Dbugs*.

A new spelling of words has had to come in, phonetic, and now all textbooks are printed in 'new Tibetan'. These textbooks are translations of textbooks used in Shanghai secondary schools and colleges. Standard Tibetan is now being created, just as standard Chinese was created, through the revolutionary process, based on the language of the common people, so that writing and speaking now correspond to each other. As Chinese had to abandon the classical language, and write down the spoken language by creating fiction and newspaper articles in this spoken language, so does Tibetan today. Tibetan has to do what many other Third World languages do, phonetic borrowing. Tibetan borrows from Chinese sound-words, for instance, for the word 'communism'.

Standard Tibetan will be based on the Lhasa spoken language, and will be used everywhere in China where there are Tibetans. Thirty Shanghai educators have come to Lhasa to help in the compilation of a dictionary, and in each autonomous district there are teams of Tibetan and Han scholars also working on the dictionary. 'The language is becoming the creative language of the workers and peasants of Tibet,' said the director.

But meanwhile, and because the leap into the future has been so swift in Tibet, it is clear that the Han (standard Chinese) language must be taught and used for higher education, especially for Tibetan students attending inland universities. This means that many cadres in Tibet will perforce become bilingual, not a bad thing in itself.

I visited the chemistry laboratory, where the cheerful, noisy students were making experiments to produce sulphuric acid. On the wall was the Mendelian table of elements, and the students have to learn them: Hg for mercury, Au for gold, Cu for copper; both the Han and the Tibetan equivalents were placed below the symbol. 'But we do not teach them English yet; they have enough to do with learning Han on top of the Tibetan,' said the director.

He asked me how such problems were tackled in Europe, for he had seen a report of some demands by certain groups for cultural equality. 'Perhaps we can learn something from them.' 'I think they might learn something from you,' I replied, wondering if, one day, the problem of teaching astrophysics in Celtic would crop up.

There are now twenty secondary (middle schools) with lower and upper levels in Tibet, and nine vocational training schools. Five thousand students have graduated from the Lhasa Middle School since 1964. The upper-middle year will add a department of agricultural science, to orient future cadres towards the countryside. 'We also plan to become at least 50 per cent self-sufficient economically, like the "work and study" schools in Chinese provinces.' This was in order to fulfil the 'self-reliance' policy. 'We also have to produce our own teachers, many more.' Integration with practical work was now pushed vigorously. 60 students were at the cement factory, learning about concrete. 30 had gone to the high plateaux to learn improved sheep breeding. Another 30 were with a PLA team, learning better methods of raising cattle. About 20 were at the Lhasa hospital, and 27 were working at the newspaper, the *Tibet Daily*, in Lhasa city.

The *Tibet Daily* is bilingual. I visited the printing press, the neat, functional quarters where Han and Tibetan staff live.

There was no printing of books in Tibet before 1959. In the monasteries, wooden blocks were used, daubed with soot or ochre for black or red. The printing done with these engraved woodblocks was all religious, and done by the monks. There

were no journalists, no tradition of reading or writing literature. Young nobles who had gone to English schools sent for
newspapers from India, which came by yak's back over the
passes.

The designing of type-moulds for the Tibetan language was
started in 1951-2, and typecasting machines were made in
Peking. The first Tibetans were trained in typesetting. On
May 4, 1955, the first newspaper page ever printed in Tibet
came off the press; it was called *Brief News*, and had 3,000
copies, twice a week.

Now the Hsinhua Printing Press has established a full-scale
printing works here in Lhasa, with branches in Lindze and
Gyantze. There are teletype casting machines, and news published in the *Tibet Daily* is local, national, and international.
It is a four-page newspaper, with equal space for Han and
Tibetan. The output is round 15,000 a day; each newspaper
is probably read by more than twenty people. There are also
radio broadcasting, twice-a-day news in two languages, and
the reading out of articles and editorials of importance from
the newspaper, for those who do not read it. There are also
education, agricultural news, weather news, singing, and
opera.

Four million books have been printed in Tibet and distributed in the last ten years. They are, of course, chiefly utili-
tarian; technical, scientific, medical, and political. Mao
Tsetung, Marx, Engels and Lenin, are all in Tibetan today.
And now Chinese novels are being translated into Tibetan.

On Tibetan literature, there is little to say so far. Apart from
the oral tradition of legends and tales, and religious texts,
there are many folk poems and songs among the people, but
they were never written down. At present Tibetans in the
minority institutes are attempting to write short pieces,
novelettes, poems, and it is not impossible to imagine a 'best-
seller' from Tibetan translated into Han.

As for telephone lines, the telephone was already working between Peking and Lhasa in 1956. A network of long-distance

phone lines is covering the whole hinterland, and all of Tibet's main cities are linked by telephone.

In my room in the guesthouse, a China-made radio set sat on the writing desk. I could hear, very clearly, not only the local broadcasts, but also the BBC, Radio-Pakistan, All-India Radio, and broadcasts from the USSR. Also, of course, Peking, and even Japan. The utter clearness of radio receiving is probably due to the fact that Tibet is 'the roof of the world'.

The Tibetans are wonderful dancers and singers. Spontaneously, at any time, they will burst into song, and start dancing. Their cadenced suppleness, ease of movement, is something which the Hans admire greatly. During my stay, I saw three excellent performances, given by amateur troupes from the communes. Each commune, each village, has its 'cultural team'. The dancers and singers were young people, and all of them worked; this was their spare-time hobby. Even though the themes enacted were occasionally strongly political, they were done with humour and natural grace, and were very entertaining. All China is now becoming 'Tibetanized'; no primary school, kindergarten, or nursery, from far Manchuria to the deep south of Canton, is without its 'Tibetan songs and dances', taught to the children. The Hans know that foot-binding, and Confucian prudery, grievously damaged their dancing ability. It is through the national minorities that they are rediscovering these arts.

But the old religious music, the haunting chant of psalms, the blowing of great horns to ensure that devils should leave the valley, will probably not be heard again.

Thus, Tibet today; ebullient, and directed towards its own future prosperity. One can only reflect on the wisdom of the leaders of China, who saw clearly that the best unity is not monolithic cultural conformism, but diversity. There is no fear, no cowering servility, but an atmosphere of mutual trust and respect, which is very impressive. This proud, intelligent and beautiful race seems to have come into its own. In the streets, the few and rare policemen to direct the traffic carry no weapons, nor are there any patrols, or barbed wire, or enclosures except round the young trees. I can scarcely believe that here, in Tibet, that most backward and hermetic of regions, the leap from the seventh to the twentieth century has been made in one generation. I can only set down what I see: that a new generation is taking the future in its own hands, and that it is Tibetan.

9

A Wall of Bronze

The wind. A blinding, lacerating blizzard of sand and stone, and the whole world destroyed by this maelstrom of small pebbles whirling in the choking air. Lips, hands and face are flayed. The turquoise sky, the white houses, even the Potala, are no longer there, all swallowed in a yellow opaqueness which is the wind.

For three days the wind blew, and no planes came. 'Winter is coming,' said my hosts. This is the time when children die, for they cannot breathe; and when pneumonia is rife.' The scant oxygen is further reduced.

Then, relief. With night the wind abates though an overhang of sand will remain in the air for another day or more. In the past, the lamas of Iron Hill blew long silver trumpets to compel the wind away. Cold darkness clutches at the valley, and the first ice is upon the river's edge till noon.

My hosts are very kind to me. Political Commissar Jen Yung, and his second in command Tien Pao, have both received me to dinner, and again to lunch; we have talked, and we have drunk both *maotai* and also Tibetan barley liquor, fermented and sweet. Talk is smooth, civilized, precise.

Long Marchers (I have met a good many of them in my peregrinations through China) are the most self-effacing, modest, soft-spoken people one could meet. All of them have fantastic lives behind them; many have extraordinary work in front of them. But not one of them thinks of himself as a hero. The word would make them uneasy. They never think of 'I'. They always say 'we', meaning the people they serve.

Jen Yung, Tien Pao, and also round-faced, quiet Ch'iao, are 'the children' of the Long March; those stout-hearted small boys who followed the Red soldiers; they were then 13, 14, 15 ... the adult soldiers carried them on their shoulders across the rivers. They acted as stretcher bearers for the wounded, they prepared food, they sang and danced in skits performed in the villages through which the Red Army passed ... their whole lives have been moulded by this experience. They are compelling because they never try to impress.

Jen Yung is tall, handsome, looks forty-five and is in his sixties. In the theatre, when we watch a performance, sitting in the front row, he gets up at least three or four times to pass sweets to the children in other rows, or to talk to one or other person in the audience. Ch'iao, after a meeting or a talk, quietly empties the ashtrays and plumps back the chair cushions, like any room attendant. Tien Pao, after a talk with me, sits down informally upon the carpet and swaps stories and plays cards with the lorry drivers who have come on the long journeys from the inland. This is not a show. They are just made that way.

I feel that these men, here in Tibet, are a very good choice. For they are not out for power; they are doing their best to train Tibetans, especially the young, to take their places. I have noticed that the generation that is taking over is between 29 and 37 years old, with the largest number between 33 and 34.

I meet Jedi, also in the revolutionary committee, and Party secretary, so handsome that I stare. Jedi is in his early thirties; he is the son of a slave herdsman, and tells me about the high plateaux of Ali, 4·5 kilometres to 5 kilometres high. 'You must come there next time ... there are yaks, sheep, and horses, the most beautiful horses.' Everything Jedi learnt he learnt when the PLA came to the high plateaux and the herdsmen were liberated. Looking at Jedi, I feel the banked fire and passion under his mild, polite exterior, and suddenly the word liberation takes on weight and power. People like Jedi are New Tibet. 'Where would I be, what would we the people of Tibet be like, if Chairman Mao and the Revolution had not come to us?' says Jedi. 'There is no future for us except in our great common motherland. The imperialists have tried to separate us for a long time. But that was only to swallow us piecemeal.'

Tien Pao repeats the essential policy: to train cadres of Tibetan nationality for Tibet. He also tells me that the 'triple alliance' between old, middle-aged and young, is implemented in all the committees and factories, at all levels; and of course women, in a proportion of at least 30 per cent, must be at all levels in all the committees.

'Only Chairman Mao's policies towards national minorities could solve the contradictions, both chauvinism and localism,' says Tien Pao. He reminds me that Tibet has four central committee members and two alternates, and members in the standing committee of the National Peoples' Congress. Two central committee members are women, Pasang and Yan Tsung. 'But our young people are modest and unchanged by their elevation into leadership.'

Because of the wind, everyone is worried that I may not have enough to do (they have noticed that I am an active person) and so bridge is suggested (my bouts of gin-rummy with the airport manager in Chengtu, nine years ago, have been duly noted!) So we play bridge one night, and forget the wind. Ch'iao is a magnificent bridge player, and we have my friend Hsin Chiang, who has come from Peking with me, and Comrade Wang, from Shanghai. Ch'iao is unbeatable. He makes three no trumps whatever the cards; I am content to play dummy and we win. 'Where did you learnt to play such good bridge? Surely not during the Long March.' Comrade Ch'iao smiles shyly. 'I just picked it up.'

Now is the time for questions, many questions come to mind. Where is the Panchen Lama? People abroad have been wondering about his fate. They will ask me. Some say he has been liquidated.

My hosts smile. Oh no, that is not our way. The Panchen Lama is at present studying in Peking.

The word study has many implications. It is clear that the Panchen Lama is no longer a political force; but it is also clear to me that his presence here would continue to stir up the embers of religious absolutism. Who knows but that one day, like the ex-emperor, Pu Yi, he will return ... but he will have changed very much, and Tibet will also have changed very much.

Another question: what if the Dalai Lama should ask to return to Tibet?

'Some of those in the Dalai Lama's entourage, who went away with him, have now returned,' is the reply. 'We have welcomed them.' In September 1975 Mr Hua Kuo-feng, leading the delegation of the Central Government to celebrate in Lhasa the tenth anniversary of Tibet's autonomy, had referred to the 'criminal actions of the treacherous Dalai Lama clique', but added that those who returned would be forgiven, whatever they had done. 'If after returning, they want to leave, we let them leave,' I was also told.

As for the Dalai Lama himself, I have heard recently – but it may be only a rumour – that he wants to give up being a Living God, and retire into private life – but that his entourage would not allow this, as it would be the end of the myth they sustained (and derived benefit from) for so many years.[1]

What about defence? What about this vast frontier which, however mountainous, is not impassable?

On matters of defence, the past has shown that Tibet was not invulnerable to invasion; on this score 'we have no illusions'. In the 1960s, when the border clashes with India occurred, both the United States and Japan were hostile to China; and the USSR would also move into the position of enemy. I had an interview with the late Premier Chou En-lai, in which he told me that China *might* be attacked by all four countries together; but 'we have made full preparations taking this into account.'

But in the 1970s the world had changed. The CIA, which had supported the armed Khampas and the Dalai Lama regime abroad for so many years, wound up this 'operation' in 1972, when President Nixon went to China. No more money, no more weapons, and no more parachuting of Khampas trained at Camp Hale, Colorado, into Tibet. Anyway these parachute drops had proved total disasters. Some border raids had been attempted, even filmed, for publicity, but did not make any impact. The last one occurred in 1969. The Indian government continued training some Tibetans in India as late as 1974. But by then most of the Tibetans had gone into petty trade and had no stomach for any fighting. Then in 1974 King Birendra of Nepal sent an army to root out the last remnants of the Khampas—become bandits—from remote areas in Nepal. In June 1976 King Birendra was to visit Tibet officially, and a railway and airline to Kathmandu is in the offing; meantime the Indian government, too, has moved towards better relations with China.

In August 1975 a small frontier clash occurred between an Indian army patrol and a Chinese garrison on the frontier. Fire was exchanged, four Indian soldiers were killed. An official statement of the Ministry of Foreign Affairs in Peking came out three months later, on October 19. It tersely gave an account of the event, and also of the fact that a receipt for the four bodies of the Indian soldiers had been issued by the Indian Chargé d'Affaires in Peking, and the bodies repatriated; the Indians had penetrated into Chinese territory.

There was no furore in India, and later, in Delhi, an unofficial Indian friend would tell me: 'You realize that, had we wanted to, we could have mobilized a million demonstrators (at a couple of rupees each) to shout some slogans in front of the Chinese Embassy in New Delhi ... but we did not do a thing.' This restraint was duly noted both in Peking and in Lhasa. The only country which kept on for some weeks accusing China of 'aggression' and 'invasion of Indian territory' was the USSR.

It is improbable, therefore, that a concerted attack on China will occur; in fact, Europe is in far greater danger of a massive offensive deployment from the USSR than is China. But 'we remain vigilant'.

By its geographical situation, Tibet is of extreme strategic importance; it is the very heart of Asia, the advance post of China's south-west, a bastion of colossal size, dominating the hinterland. Its defence is of decisive importance to China. Prime Minister Hua Kuo-feng laid stress upon defence 'against the activities of aggression and subversion by social-imperialism ... ' meaning the USSR.

As in China, defence in Tibet is at several levels. At the level of the people, the policies of autonomy, of self-reliance, the accelerated economic development, the financial support for swift industrial expansion, and the promotion of Tibet's own cadres at all levels are the very foundation of defence. A hostile population is the enemy within; an enthusiastic population, at one with the policies of its leaders, is the decisive factor. 'What is our true wall of bronze? It is the people,' said Mao Tsetung many decades ago. 'Man not weapons decides the issue of war.' In September 1975 Tien Pao, in a speech in Lhasa, called upon Tibet to 'build this wall of bronze'. 'We are in the process of doing things that our forebears never attempted, following a road they never took,' he added, quoting Mao Tsetung.

As everywhere else in China, there is a people's militia in Tibet, at commune level, at factory level. In 1962, when the Indian army attacked on the frontier, they found themselves already confronted by the beginnings of a Tibetan militia. The Tibetans acted as food suppliers, as stretcher bearers and helpers to the PLA. Tibetan stretcher bearers at first refused to pick up the Indian wounded; in the past they were used to finishing them off. 'Only when we explained to them Chairman Mao's policy towards the captured and the wounded did they pick them up.' 800 Indian wounded were treated at hospitals in Tibet and then sent back to India, with arms and equipment intact.

Militia training, on the high plateaux, among the herdsmen,

in the factories, is visible. Besides that, Tibetans are joining the PLA as soldiers. They are extremely good marksmen. In case of a conventional invasion, the militia has a very basic role, acting as guerrillas, harassing the enemy, denying food, cutting supplies, sabotaging ... This is people's war, conducted by people fighting on their own land.

In case of bombing, there are everywhere in China large underground cities complete with dormitories, schools, shops, bath and toilet facilities, underground hydro-electric plants ... oil pipelines, and tunnels. 'Dig tunnels deep, store grain everywhere and never seek hegemony,' is Mao's recipe for defence. Here in Tibet, with a vast amount of land and so few people, digging underground cities would be useless effort (and impossible to achieve). But there are already precautions being taken, especially round factory sites, with storing of cereals.

To pour nuclear bombs on the roof of the world would probably bring untold disaster over an immense area of Asia, and affect even large tracts of Siberia; so that precautions against nuclear bombing—though they do exist—are not as advanced as in heavily peopled centres, such as Shanghai, with ten million inhabitants. Do the Chinese have missile sites and nuclear installations in Tibet? I do not know. But it is subversion, rather than aggression, especially subversion from within, which China fights now; and it is upon the success of the policies, accelerated development, and the enthusiasm of the people themselves, that the issue of this fight will be decided.

And now had come the day of departure. I had been given some touching mementoes: a yak's tail, beautiful but so smelly that I had to request my sixth brother, in Chengtu, to boil it gently for some hours ... a magnificent album on Tibet; and a large parcel of tea planted in Tibet. It is indeed very good tea. I was also given some yak butter—which I gave away rather hastily to some friends in Szechuan—and a very fine piece of wool cloth, produced by the Lindze factory. I was told it was the same quality as that given to President Nixon when he visited China in 1972.

I took a final stroll round Lhasa. I was sad to leave. Comrade Chen, and also gentle, able photographer Chen, who had climbed Everest in the 1960s, Dr Chasi, my Tibetan doctor, and Miss Ma, the interpreter; and little Kuo, a young girl from Shansi province, who always carried my bag and my camera ... and others. I would remember them a long, long time.

There was the Jokka Kang, gleaming among the whitewashed houses. People strolled, relaxed after the wind; what a cheerful, and handsome people Tibetans are! The shops with their gay lintels, dark interiors, and painted top windows.

Night in Lhasa. Off to the cinema, to see the conquest of Everest by the Tibetan woman, Panthog, and six men. A marvellous film, so gripping, I panted with the climbers, up those nightmare ice ridges, to the bare stone peak, flayed by all the winds of the earth.

I walk back at night, in the freezing air, in the marvellous Tibetan night. Above my head, a Milky Way so enormous, so studded with gem myriads of stars, clusters of stars, stars like flowers bursting out of the sky, ready to drop into my outstretched hands ... here is a marvel even greater than that of day with its gold and turquoise when the sun seeks out every cell of one's body ... Once again that sense of levitation, of rising, rising, dissolving among the billions of ruby and sapphire stars; and sudden, absolute knowledge of one's own infinitesimal smallness. I feel like one of those sand specks in the wind of space, whirling in a pebbled universe of nebulae, all specks, dust. I raise both arms to catch and grip the sky. Paradise.

And here is the Potala, small, placid, in the starlight. Inoffensive proud stone, insignificant its beauty, and its evil, too. And on the road, blinking against the headlights of a passing lorry, comes a man, muffled in a pale leather cloak, and singing to himself, going home.

Notes

1 Tibet and the Time Machine

1 Han – name the 'typical' Chinese give to themselves. There are fifty-five nationalities in China, the Han being one but in an overwhelming majority: 92 per cent against 8 per cent for all the other 54, including the Tibetans.
2 See Han Suyin, *The Crippled Tree* (Cape, London, 1965).
3 Also spelt Khamba.
4 Stuart and Roma Gelder, *The Timely Rain* (Hutchinson, London, 1964).
5 See p. 2; also map of Tibet, *The Times Atlas of China*, ed. Denis C. Twitchett and P. J. M. Geelan (Times Newspapers, London, 1974), pp. 109–11.
6 The Nepalese princess was also a Buddhist, and is also credited with influencing her husband to adopt the religion.
7 After having, briefly, invaded Nepal.
8 M. Huc, *Travels in Tartary, Thibet and China* (Nelson, London, 1856).
9 See Gelder, *The Timely Rain*, p. 33.
10 A. L. Strong, *Tibetan Interviews* (Foreign Language Press, Peking, 1959), p. 41.
11 Alan Winnington, *Tibet* (Lawrence & Wishart, London, 1957).
12 Huc, *Travels in Tartary*.
13 The child who was not chosen is now an accountant in a Tibetan commune.
14 See p. 3. The present fourteenth Dalai Lama has an elder brother, who was the High Abbot of the Kumbum monastery, Tsinghai province. He fled in 1951 and has been living in the United States.
15 Fosco Maraini, *Tibet Secret* (Arthaud, Paris, 1926).
16 Winnington, *Tibet*, p. 65.
17 According to an interview in Lhasa, only 870,000 in 1949. But

this is counting only the Tsang people and excluding other nationalities in the Tibetan region.

18 Winnington, *Tibet*, p. 65.

19 According to Père Huc, 3,000 in U (eastern Tibet) alone.

20 'There is no year in which this malady does not make fearful ravages in Lhasa.' Huc, *Travels in Tartary*, p. 47.

21 VD was probably transmitted by the numerous pilgrims (see Chapter 2) as it was also rife among the Mongols.

2 Lhasa Only Yesterday

1 There are probably another million 'lamaist' believers, who identify themselves with Tibetan lamaism, in Kashmir, Sikkim, Bhutan, Nepal and India.

2 M. Huc, *Travels in Tartary, Thibet and China* (Nelson, London, 1856), pp. 412–13.

3 Alan Winnington, *Tibet* (Lawrence & Wishart, London, 1957), pp. 76, 77.

4 See G. N. Patterson's books on Tibet—*God's Fool* (Faber & Faber, London, 1956); *Peking versus Delhi* (Faber & Faber, London, 1963); *Tibetan Journey* (Faber & Faber, London, 1954).

5 F. Spencer Chapman, *Lhasa Holy City* (Chatto & Windus, London, 1938).

6 Perceval Landon, *Lhasa* (Hurst & Blackett, London, 1905).

7 Huc, *Travels in Tartary*, p. 471.

8 Winnington, *Tibet*, p. 78.

9 Stuart and Roma Gelder, *The Timely Rain* (Hutchinson, London, 1964), pp. 79, 80.

10 These will have latrines, and a modern system of purified running water. One can, if clinging to the exotic, regret that the new houses will probably be in the functional Chinese architecture. However, beautiful old houses belonging to the Tibetan nobility are being kept, cleaned and repaired.

11 See p. 114.

12 In the 1920s Lhasa had no more than 10,000 'fixed' inhabitants, but around 40,000 monks in the monasteries.

13 Landon, *Lhasa*, quoted in Gelder, *The Timely Rain*.

14 Reported in 1957. In 1964 Gelder told me it was 14,000 lbs a week in 1962.

15 There were never more than three to four hundred lamas living at the Jokka Kang. There are now a dozen.

16 See further, pp. 39–40.

17 Every nobleman-landlord also had the right to inflict 'justice' upon his retainers, serfs and slaves.

18 Although according to some 'witnesses' (Tibetan refugees in India who had left Tibet with the Dalai Lama) they had also been partly destroyed.

19 Stuart Gelder told me that a lamp was kept burning in front of the Dalai Lama's photograph when he visited the Norbulingka in 1962, three years after the Dalai Lama's departure.

20 Shanks's vitreous china.

21 October 19, 1975. See further, p. 159.

22 Austin Waddell, *Lhasa and its Mysteries* (Methuen, London, 1906).

23 As previously related, Tibetans overflowed the Himalayas, and they are found in Kashmir (Leh, Ladakh), Nepal, Sikkim, Bhutan, and large tracts of north-east India. Possibly a million or more Tibetans thus live south of their border.

24 See *The Times*'s reports by Perceval Landon, 1904, and *Lhasa*.

25 The area of Kantze, where the Khampas come from, and which was part of Szechuan from the seventeenth century, was also incorporated in Sikang province. In 1955, the Chamdo region was restored to Tibet by the Central Government.

26 Into Inner and Outer Tibet; this meant that the Chamdo area would remain Chinese; Tibet proper would be 'autonomous' under British 'protection'.

27 Alistair Lamb, *Asian Frontiers, Studies in a Continuing Problem* (Praeger, New York, 1968), pp. 124–5.

28 For further interesting sidelights on this subject, consult Karunakar Gupta, *The Hidden History of the Sino-Indian Frontier* (Minerva, Calcutta, 1974). The courageous Mr Gupta reveals how the legal basis for the McMahon line lay in the Simla agreement of 1913–14, and the Simla Convention, which, because the Chinese refused to sign or ratify it, had no binding value in international law. The British government (and the Indian government under Great Britain) at the time so concluded, and continued to be of this view when, in 1929–33, a new edition of the standard work on British Indian treaties, *Aitchison's Treaties*, was reissued. In vol. XIV of that series it is made quite clear that

the Simla Convention was abortive because the Chinese refused
to sign it. However, a substitution then took place in London:
another vol. xiv was issued to replace the original, on the advice
of Sir Olaf Caroe, but under the same date as the original. This
substitution managed to confuse the issue even more, but the
India Office, when it substituted a new 'revised' vol. xiv (though
under the same date) forgot that the original vol. xiv was still in
existence, for instance at Harvard. Recently the Kraus Reprint
Company reissued the entire 1929–33 edition of *Aitchison*, repro-
ducing the Harvard original, rather than the spurious 'original'
which replaced it and which is in London.

29 Gyantze. See map, p. xi.
30 Winnington, *Tibet*, p. 212.
31 Sir Charles Bell, *Portrait of the Dalai Lama* (1946).
32 Heinrich Harrer, *Seven Years in Tibet*, trans. R. Graves (Hart
Davis, London, 1953). Mr Harrer was also a friend of the Dalai
Lama's elder brother, who was the Abbot of Kumbum monastery, in Tsinghai province, and who departed for American in
1951.
33 Lowell Thomas Jr, *Out of this World* (Macdonald, London,
1951).
34 Ngapo Nawang Jigme is today vice-chairman of the standing committee of the National People's Congress of China,
acting chairman of the revolutionary committee for the Autonomous Region of Tibet, and deputy commander of the PLA in
Tibet.
35 A. L. Strong, *Tibetan Interviews* (Foreign Language Press,
Peking, 1959), p. 107.
36 Ibid., pp. 105–6.
37 Ibid., p. 36. Interview with Ngapo Nawang Jigme.
38 Besides, Nehru had the bitter experience of partition, and the
United States were openly favouring Pakistan, pouring money
and weapons into the new Muslim state.
39 See map in Lamb, *Asian Frontiers*, p. 120.

3 Rifles in the Rice Heap – The Insurrection of 1959

1 Out of every 100 lorries, 30 carried the fuel necessary for the
journey.

2 Alan Winnington, *Tibet* (Lawrence & Wishart, London, 1957), p. 68.

3 Interview by author with a former serf road-worker, now at commune cadre.

4 See p. 75.

5 The three largest monasteries in Lhasa valley.

6 Interview with former lama, but of low class, Tzumen Jendze.

7 Perceval Landon, *Lhasa* (Hurst & Blackett, London, 1905).

8 A. L. Waddell, *The Buddhism of Tibet or Lamaism* (Heffers, Cambridge, 1895).

9 F. Spencer Chapman, *Lhasa Holy City* (Chatto & Windus, London, 1938).

10 The author interviewed sixty Tibetans—ex-serfs, ex-slaves, workers, women, herdsmen, doctors, as well as lamas like Tzumen Jendze.

11 Robert Ford, the English radio operator captured in Tibet, also testified to the correct behaviour of the PLA. See his book, *Captured in Tibet* (Harrap, London, 1957).

12 Save for a small area in Inner Mongolia and border areas with Kashmir and Afghanistan.

13 See Gelder, *The Timely Rain*, pp. 204-5.

14 Unlike the British aristocracy, trade and commerce were the almost exclusive employment of nobles and also of many lamas. The Kantze (Khampa) district had 'two lamas for every layman', all actively engaged in trade. These Khampas subsequently filtered into east Tibet, and the monasteries provided refuge for them. See G. N. Patterson, *Peking versus Delhi* (Faber & Faber, London, 1963), pp. 159-61.

15 But Kantze, the Khampa region, which had also been incorporated in Sikang province, was restored to Szechuan, since it had been part of Szechuan since the seventeenth century.

16 Serf revolts were by no means uncommon in the past, and there is probably truth in the Dalai Lama's complaint that uprisings against exactions occurred.

17 Winnington, *Tibet*, p. 218.

18 It was opened in 1955. Visited by the author. It is now Lhasa's largest Secondary School or High School.

19 Although the Dalai Lama later said he had tried to make reforms, and had been hindered—by the preparatory committee!

20 Winnington, *Tibet*, p. 226.
21 The name CIA is deliberately not used by the author. For a fuller account see *Far Eastern Economic Review* (September 15, 1975), pp. 30, 31.
22 See further, p. 119.
23 Documents captured by the PLA in the headquarters of the Tibetan rebels: Hsinhua, Lhasa, April 27, 1959. The proclamation was also sent to Kalimpong in India to be broadcast.
24 *Concerning the Question of Tibet* (Foreign Language Press, Peking, 1959), pp. 166–7.

4 *The Serfs*

1 Interview with leading officials. See Chapter 9.
2 The Memba district is one of five comprising one of the other ethnic groups of Tibet.
3 Alan Winnington reported this as happening along the road built through Chamdo territory to Lhasa in 1956. *Tibet* (Lawrence & Wishart, London, 1957), pp. 66–8.
4 See map, p. xi.
5 Author's figures, checked from the revolutionary museum in Lhasa, say 120,000. Winnington's figures may include Tibetan monks in other provinces of China, or even in Ladakh (Kashmir) and other areas outside China.
6 There were, in 1974, 1,640,000 people in Tibet, of whom 96 per cent are Tsang (Tibetan), which makes 1,574,000 'Tibetans'; the remaining approximately 100,000 being Loba, Memba and Hui groups. There are probably 250,000 Hans in Tibet, comprising the PLA garrisons along the very long frontiers with India, Pakistan and Soviet Russia, cadres, teachers, doctors, engineers, workers, etc. Other estimates are of 300,000 Hans: not a large figure if one realizes the strategic importance of the region and the very long frontiers—about 2,000 kilometres, or more.
7 Winnington, *Tibet*, pp. 165–8. I use these figures because they appear more dispassionate than those of Anna Louise Strong in 1959; but Miss Strong has made some very accurate observations on ula.
8 See Han Suyin, *Wind in the Tower* (Cape, London, 1976).

9 The Panchen Lama cooperated with the new regime till 1964. See Chapter 9.

10 Speech of Tien Pao – Lhasa, September 7, 1975, on the occasion of the celebration of Tibet's tenth year of autonomy.

11 Necessary due to the winds which sweep Tibetan valleys.

12 Tsushui county has a town of 3–4,000 inhabitants, with industrial development. The Hans concentrate still in the cities (Lhasa, Shigatze, Chamdo, Nachu, etc.).

13 Tachai brigade in Shansi province, China, is *the* model for agriculture.

14 Said to me by Jen Yung, Political Commissar for the Tibet region.

15 The agricultural tax in Tibet works out at 4·5 per cent of the harvest.

16 It was hopeless to ask how many of each. I could only find out that 'more than half' were sheep.

5 *The New Magic of Medicine*

1 As described by previous travellers to Tibet.

2 Alan Winnington in 1955, *Tibet* (Lawrence & Wishart, London, 1957), pp. 205–11.

3 This is part of the complex struggle in China which culminated in the Cultural Revolution. See Han Suyin, *Wind in the Tower* (Cape, London, 1976).

4 The birth rate is 40 per 1,000 in rural areas, 19 per 1,000 in Lhasa city, because Lhasa has many cadres, both Han and Tibetan.

5 The average works out at 49·6 per cent males and 51·4 per cent females. Women also live longer now than men do, despite the fact that they are still the 'heavy labour' force.

6 Horns and pelts, glands and hoofs, of various animals.

6 *The Birth of the Worker – New Lhasa*

1 All spinning and weaving of finer cloth was done by men.

2 See Alan Winnington, *Tibet* (Lawrence & Wishart, London, 1957), p. 176.

3 The Dalai Lama's subsequent charge that reforms were impeded

by the Han Chinese does not stand up after an examination of the facts.

4 See map, p. xi, for main roads in Tibet. Lindze (Nyingchi) now has a dozen various factories linked by road with Nachu, Shigatze, Chamdo and the Ali plateau – the road convoys carry wool, hides and metals.

5 See map, p. xi.

6 See Chapter 7.

7 Taching oilfield in Manchuria, a 'model' for industrialization as Tachai is for agricultural development.

8 Two of the canteens are for the families of workers and one for Muslim Tibetans.

9 See Han Suyin, *Wind in the Tower* (Cape, London, 1976).

10 M. Huc, *Travels in Tartary, Thibet and China* (Nelson, London, 1856), p. 419.

11 Lungochoka learnt to read and write in the monastery.

12 Tuberculous glands in the neck were very common, due to the infected milk.

13 Since June 1976 a railway and an airline to Kathmandu, Nepal, have been projected, and another road, which took nine years to complete, from Yunnan province, has been opened.

7 A Kingdom of Women

1 See *An Historical Atlas of China* (Edinburgh University Press and Djambatan N.V., Amsterdam, 1966), p. 31, 'China in A.D. 750'.

2 As a result, no canals were dug. Perhaps that is why in the countryside I saw so many *women* digging canals today, proving themselves 'equal to men' by this gesture.

3 This custom was copied from Confucian China.

4 Alan Winnington, *Tibet* (Lawrence & Wishart, London, 1957), pp. 101–2.

8 Education and Autonomy

1 'Under the unified leadership of the Central Government autonomous leadership organizations (now revolutionary committees) possess the functions and powers of local government organizations. They possess autonomous rights on finance,

economy, culture, education, public security and organization of local popular forces (militia).

'The language spoken and written by the local nationalities is the *official* language of the autonomous region.

'The Central Government must protect the rights of the autonomous units and help them to train and promote cadres of the minority nationalities and also promote their cultural and economic development, to reinforce unity among the various nationalities, and their active participation in the leadership of all affairs of the State, so that they will contribute to the development of the autonomous region and to the progress of the Chinese Revolution.'

2 A change to the Cyrillic alphabet in the early 1950s was unsuccessful. In 1970 the Uighurs, whose language is closely related to Turkish, decided to adopt the Roman alphabet — as the Turks have done.

3 Han Suyin, *Wind in the Tower* (Cape, London, 1976).

4 'State-granted funds have made up the greater part of the region's revenue ... Since 1960 the amount spent by the State on farmland, water and conservancy projects, public health, culture and education in rural areas, and disease-prevention measures for livestock, as well as relief, is four times the amount of taxes collected in the region ...

'So that the economy, culture and education may progress more rapidly, the State practises a policy of lightening taxation ... and favourable treatment as regards the purchase of material. Taxes in Tibet are far lower than the national average; for instance, products of national industry ... are taxed only one-tenth of the national average. Since 1959, the State has increased by 30 to 100 per cent the purchasing price of Tibet's principal agricultural products [when sold to the State — author's note] and also of its livestock and other specialities, and has lowered from 30 to 75 per cent the price of products for agricultural and livestock sold to Tibet, as well as that of light industrial goods sold to the local population.'

Speech by Tien Pao, vice-chairman of the revolutionary committee for the Tibet Autonomous Region, September 7, 1975, in Lhasa. Hsinhua News Service.

5 Apa Tibetan Autonomous District, Szechuan province.

6 See Han Suyin, 'The Long March', *The Morning Deluge* (Cape, London, 1972).
7 There are seven nationalities in Sinkiang of which the Kazakhs are one.
8 Stuart and Roma Gelder visited this school in 1962. See *The Timely Rain* (Hutchinson, London, 1964), p. 167.
9 Meaning that it had an elitist orientation.

9 *A Wall of Bronze*

1 From a United Nations' official, not Chinese.

Bibliography

F. Spencer Chapman, *Lhasa Holy City* (Chatto & Windus, London, 1938).

Stuart and Roma Gelder, *The Timely Rain* (Hutchinson, London, 1964).

M. Huc, *Travels in the Chinese Empire* (Harper Bros, New York, 1878).

M. Huc, *Travels in Tartary, Thibet and China* (Nelson, London, 1856).

Alistair Lamb, *Asian Frontiers: Studies in a Continuing Problem* (Praeger, New York, 1968).

Alistair Lamb, *The China–India Border* (Chatham House Essays, London, 1964).

Alistair Lamb, 'The Indo-Tibetan Border', *Australian Journal of Politics and History*, vol. VI, no. 1 (May 1960).

Alistair Lamb, 'Tibet in Anglo-Chinese Relations, 1767–1842', *Journal of Royal Asiatic Society* (October 1957 and April 1958).

Perceval Landon, *Lhasa* (Hurst & Blackett, London, 1905).

Fosco Maraini, *Tibet Secret* (Arthaud, Paris, 1926).

Neville Maxwell, *India's China War* (Cape, London, 1970).

George N. Patterson, *God's Fool* (Faber & Faber, London, 1956).

George N. Patterson, *Peking versus Delhi* (Faber & Faber, London, 1963).

George N. Patterson, *Tibetan Journey* (Faber & Faber, London, 1954).

Anna Louise Strong, *Tibetan Interviews* (Foreign Language Press, Peking, 1959).

Anna Louise Strong, *When Serfs Stood Up in Tibet* (Central Books, London, 1960).

Thubten Jigme Norbu, Abbot of Kumbum, *Tibet is my Country* (details not known).

A. L. Waddell, *The Buddhism of Tibet or Lamaism* (Heffers, Cambridge, 1895).

Alan Winnington, *Tibet* (Lawrence & Wishart, London, 1957).

China Reconstructs: Special Supplement (Peking, November 1959).

An Historical Atlas of China (Edinburgh University Press and Djambatan N.V., Amsterdam, 1966).

Letter of Prime Minister Chou En-lai to all Leaders of Asian and African Countries on the Question of the Sino-Indian Border (Peking, November 15, 1962).

The Prime Minister on Sino-Indian Relations (Jawarhalal Nehru), vols I and II (Ministry of External Affairs, New Delhi, 1958–62).

'The Revolution in Tibet and Nehru's Philosophy', Editorial Department, *People's Daily* (May 6, 1959).

The Times Atlas of China, ed. Denis C. Twitchett and P. J. M. Geelan (Times Newspapers, London, 1974).

Index